PROPORTIONAL FORM

FURTHER STUDIES IN THE SCIENCE OF BEAUTY, BEING SUPPLE-
MENTAL TO THOSE SET FORTH IN "NATURE'S
HARMONIC UNITY"

BY

SAMUEL COLMAN, N.A.

AND

C. ARTHUR COAN, LL.B.·

AUTHORS OF " NATURE'S HARMONIC UNITY," ETC

THE DRAWINGS AND CORRELATING DESCRIPTIONS ARE BY MR. COLMAN
THE TEXT AND MATHEMATICS ARE BY CAPT. COAN

G. P. PUTNAM'S SONS
NEW YORK AND LONDON
The Knickerbocker Press
1920

The Knickerbocker Press, New York

To
ALL STUDENTS OF BEAUTY
PAST AND PRESENT

CONTENTS

[1] These chapters are taken from *The Great Modules*, C. A. Coan, 1914.

ILLUSTRATIONS AND DIAGRAMS[1]

Folio numbers in Roman refer to the pages upon which diagrams and minor illustrations appear; those in Italics refer to the pages upon which major illustrations are described in the text.

[1] The illustrations are by Mr. Colman except where otherwise indicated below or in the work itself. The diagrams are by Capt. Coan.

vii

Illustrations

Illustrations

Illustrations

THE COAL SACK

A S the brightest lights cast the deepest shadows, so, also, in the most thickly star-studded spaces of the heavens, we shall find the blackest depths of emptiness. In the mid-path of the Milky Way glows the familiar Northern Cross, and barely off the glistening outlines of the cross, between alpha, gamma, and epsilon, Cygni, we shall, if we are not careful, slip into astronomy's bottomless pit, which has been familiarly nick-named "the Coal Sack," doubtless because it appears so deep and so black and so devoid of stars. So, frequently, it is in research. Where the beam of knowledge is brilliant, there, perhaps, will be found Coal Sacks in which the only light is Theory's flickering candle, always promising to blaze up into definite certainty, but, meanwhile, in constant danger of being blown out.

Since man's maturity, few subjects have received more constant attention than those leading to creation of the beautiful, whether in music, in art, in painting, in architecture, or wherever beauty may be thought to lodge. Here, if anywhere, the light of knowledge is beating in ever increasing brilliance. Here, if anywhere, research has expended itself. Yet here, in the centre of so much knowledge we find our ebon coal sack as surely as in the constellation of Cygnus. In science, we must know the factors and understand every reaction, becoming expert in predicating exact conclusions upon exact causes, but in matters pertaining to the beautiful we have fallen into the rut of assuming that, because genius and imagination were largely inspired, so they brooked no guidance nor conformed to law nor reason. So perhaps, the fault is largely our own. In the celestial Coal Sack it was long assumed that no stars shone. This, upon investigation, proves incorrect. Stars are there for the seeking, but they must be sought, being outshone by the myriads in the Milky Way. Likewise, in the subject we would pursue, knowledge exists and facts sufficient to induce greater knowledge, shadowed, notwithstanding by the glare of the lights all around.

In the final analysis, beauty shows herself in a manner surprisingly allied to mathematics, for no medium exists through which beauty can be disclosed to the senses but depends ultimately upon *proportion* for its success. Does the beauty lie in colour or sound? Both of these depend quite entirely upon the laws of proportion. Is the beauty one of form or motion? Still more intimately are these connected with the proportional laws. Since one cannot produce genius, the best that can be done is to study those laws which even genius cannot successfully defy.

Having laid claim to these theories and their furtherance in *Nature's Harmonic Unity*, it is not enough here merely to restate these claims, nor to satisfy ourselves with putting a little new wine into old bottles, taking the short cut of preparing a brief sequel to the former work. It is incumbent on us to show even more clearly and forcibly than before, these facts and the proofs upon which our theories are based, and to add to their weight new matter of value if we would warrant a new work on the subject. Since the publication of the former treatise, the lights have increased in the Coal Sack and many other works have appeared touching directly or indirectly on the questions involved, nor have we ourselves, been for a moment idle. To simplify what was said in our preceding work, to add disclosures, to clarify, to consolidate, if possible, to illuminate! These express our purpose and our hope.

As before, the plan holds strictly to the unfolding of the subject in its simplest form. To use plain every-day terms "understanded of the people," to go out of the way if necessary in order to explain by arithmetical means, things perhaps more readily and briefly and beautifully embodied in an equation or formula which, from its very effective simplicity would be as Greek or Chinese to a number of readers deserving of better treatment. It is recognised that this non-technical method presents infinite difficulties and requires infinite pains, but, against this, it presents also, infinite possibilities.

Let us forestall a few criticisms by making a brief statement covering points continually arising:

No futile claim is advanced that natural phenomena do not constantly combine to produce varying effects, nor that all examples of a class selected for study would in every point coincide with the perfect or conventionalised forms. The wonder is that, in spite of torsions and minute local variations arising from transitory causes, *Nature adheres so tenaciously to whatever form she adopts.* The point of interest is, not that no two snow crystals are alike, but that they all are, all have been, and all will be, six cornered in decoration.

Caustic criticism to the effect that Nature is not to be restricted by measurements, is wasted. Nature is restricted to certain means, whatever they may be. She does not call these by names, but we, in our finite littleness, have to do so, and whether we name them chemistry or optics or gravity or just plain geometry and mathematics, applicable to all sciences, is a matter of supreme indifference to her. Our duty and privilege is to learn what we can of her methods, and if she pertinaciously adheres to a line of action, to find out why she does it. Dare we assume that there is no reason?

It will doubtless be said, as of other efforts, that there is danger of "over doing the thing." Stop a moment. If a reason exists for all these things, then *every form, distance, and force in the Universe is a legitimate subject for research*, and each holds a lesson if we be but sharp enough to find it.

When you lay this book down, whatever your purpose be, it will involve other things than those of which we speak. So life is made up of varying interests, and it must not be thought that we feel that Nature contains nothing but proportions, nor that great progress has been made in ascertaining what the rules of these proportions are. Remember that our paths, yours and mine, cross probably but once on this subject, and that the space between the two covers of this book is all too small to say what one would say, even when it is all devoted to the subject in hand. This does not mean that we feel, or ask you to feel, that, because there is nothing else inside the covers, there is, therefore, nothing else outside.[1]

What Leonardo da Pisa and Leonardo da Vinci struggled with from a mathematical standpoint, what da Vinci and Dürer before him, Michael Angelo and a hundred others studied as artists and architects, what Hokusai in the East and Vaughn Cornish in the West saw in the waves, what Newton saw in the apple and Bently in the snow crystal, what were all these but offshoots of the same great study of Nature? What Schimper and Braun, Bravais and Sachs, Schwendener and Calandrini worked over in botany, and what Roger Cotes envisioned in his Theorems, what, after all were any of these except steps following the footprints of Conon of Samos who placed the *Coma Berenices* in the sky between the Lady and the Lion whence it could never again disappear, and who first developed a reasonable

[1] Appendix Notes, Introductory.

theory on the subject of spirals, particularly concerning that one familiarly called after his friend and co-worker Archimedes? Cook has collected data and recorded them in a way to make them enticing as well as invaluable, while Church and D'arcy Thompson also have pursued their respective ways of advancement, all adopting, of course, the background of earlier work as one necessarily must. With all of these and a thousand others at hand with their evidences and their theories it becomes more than ever impossible, if one is to get forward, to republish any lengthy examination of what has already been accomplished. If one is to add anything to the sum of human knowledge, the work may be justified in itself; and with this hope, the omission of any exhaustive review of results achieved in the past must be.accepted, nor must such an omission be construed as meaning either that these great achievements are absent from consideration or underestimated in effect. Where invaluable works of others are not so fully quoted here as this or that reader might wish, necessity compells that these be examined in their entirety elsewhere. The habit of such examination, on the whole, is wisely formed. If such theories as are here set out prove to be a modest addition to acknowledged discoveries the effort which has not been spared to present them intelligibly will have its reward. May they prove convincing.

PROPORTIONAL FORM

CHAPTER I

HEAVEN'S FIRST LAW

IN the study of Nature, man has, from time immemorial, frittered away valuable hours and years in an endeavour to visualise some almost inconceivably complex system of laws which, he took it, were necessary to explain her intricate results. Cycles and epicycles innumerable were constructed in his effort to explain astronomical phenomena, even up to the very date when at last the one basic law of gravitation was developed and he realised that it was the application and not the law itself which was complex. No science has been free from such abracadabra, and research has been correspondingly slow. Gradually and bit by bit it has been found that the mysteries of Nature yield to rules very simple when compared with the results which, in combination, they produce. Science, aided by mathematics, has step by step displaced the metaphysical guesswork of our forefathers, and the process, far from being finished, might almost be said just to have begun. The further such investigation is carried, the more clearly it appears that a few fundamental and major rules work in concert for the government of the whole scheme, and upon the universality of such a harmony and its ancient use and future value in developing beauty, was based the former treatise called *Nature's Harmonic Unity*.[1]

When years have been given to the intimate consideration of any subject, it is easily possible for the searcher to lay too much stress upon its importance, but Nature sometimes furnishes a barometer which records her wishes and needs, and calls her cohorts into action at the proper moment. She has a way of telephoning mankind a message to the effect that she feels it time he should develop a better knowledge along certain lines. Forthwith a manderin in Chinese robes, and wearing a peacock's feather, or a Thibetan priest burning incense in some walled and forbidden city, will fall into a brown study. Bent he will be on de-coding Nature's telegram, and all unaware that perhaps studious Mahometans nodding in some far-off Sahn el-Gamia and lonesome astronomers on the peaks of the Andes, explorers in the heart of Africa, anæmic students in rooms too hot, and sturdy, practical scientists in tents too cold, separated by a whole world of land and water, may have all been unconsciously impelled to take up the same questions at the self-

[1] *Nature's Harmonic Unity*, same authors (Putnam, 1912).

same time. Telepathically perhaps they will transfer to each other their agreements and disagreements preparatory to disclosing a series of inventions, discoveries, and theories which will seem in the final analysis to have come straight out of the blue. Thus, when Nature's chicks are ready to hatch, they merely peck the shell and step boldly out. In all this, you will observe that Nature has simply set the stage, rung up the curtain, spoken the prologue, and dispatched Iris as her messenger and call-girl to warn the actors of their impending cues.

A similar analogy is not lacking in the study of those laws by which Nature regulates the proportions of her works, and which it seems but logical that man should use as his guide in his own creations in art and architecture. The publication of *Nature's Harmonic Unity*, in which many of these things were treated, came after a period of long quiescence in the production of writings of this kind; yet it was scarcely in press before it was found to be surrounded by others as in a cloud. Writings came out of the east and out of the west and across the seas, all bearing on questions of the same kind, and many of these works will be found referred to in the following pages. Meanwhile, the authors of *Nature's Harmonic Unity*, continuing their original researches, have been brought to a double decision: first, that, in view of the many recent publications touching on questions of proportion in Nature, the conclusions reached in our previous work and which have happily met no inconsiderable favour, should be extended through the presentation of additional matter, and, second, as an incident, that in the new work the means of reaching those conclusions could and should be simplified in their demonstration. Hence the present book is before the public. And since the desire to simplify the labour of the reader would at once be negatived by requiring him constantly to refer to the former publication, necessity demands that while the present work is, in essence, a sequel to *Nature's Harmonic Unity*, it should nevertheless, as now presented, be in fact a complete whole, even at the expense of the repetition of certain fundamental demonstrations and principles set forth at large in the pages of the earlier writing.

Let us start then with the knowledge that, however difficult it is in any given instance to follow through the intricate mazes of any one of Nature's daily combinations, yet we may rest assured that the various rules are themselves austerely simple and each applied with religious severity. It is only the resultant combination which taxes our attention, like some confection, some marvellous creation into which we see the products of the farm, the market and the dairy poured and stirred, to be finally transmuted by a chef's magic into castles and camels and cakes, fruits and fairies and frosting.

Proportion and rule are everywhere present in Nature, and it is as hopeless to visualise her without precision as it is to imagine beauty dependent on chance, and without that order which is Heaven's first law. For, as every natural creation and phenomenon is supported and measured, guided and terminated by order and proportion, so, prone as we are to suppose that beauty is an erratic production superior to all regulation and uninfluenced by laws, yet is every form of beauty found, upon careful analysis, to be subject to the controlling power of these universal rules. One does not think of the plentiful noises of a boiler shop as music, nor does an overturned paint cart spell art; a mad and whirling brain is indeed a sad, but in no sense a beautiful thing to contemplate; and anarchy ever produces ruins and abundant chaos rather than churches, pictures, towers, and monuments. Consciously or unconsciously, beauty must have reason behind it. If this be not so, why then have we no evidence that the ape and the elephant, the horse and the faithful dog are affected by beauty equally with ourselves. Nature is founded upon laws and rules and man alone appreciates them.

> "For the world was built in order
> And the atoms march in tune."

CHAPTER II[1]

FORM AND PROPORTION

IT is frequently a matter of amazement that the human mind so quick at times to accept a natural law, should so slowly assimilate the principles logically akin to that law and which seem to follow almost on its heels, so to speak. That the great body of growing things in the vegetable kingdom are green, we know from observation; and when the scientist tells us that this is intentional and that Nature has some specific reason, we are prepared to believe him without undue question. We speculate upon what this reason may be and perhaps we conclude that, in forming an outer coating which shall readily admit those light rays most necessary to plant growth, and conversely, exclude any which might be harmful, Nature has created a covering the refraction from which produces the sensation of green to the eye. It would then follow that when growth has ceased and the plant withers and no longer cares what the light is, this coating should change to a neutral brown,— which in most instances it promptly does. That flowers requiring

[1] *From the Great Modules.* Copyrighted, 1914, by C. Arthur Coan.

6

cross-fertilisation are bright in colour or produce honey that they may draw to them those insects whose tiny wings and feet shall track the pollen over neighbouring blossoms and thus complete that circle which Nature planned, is an old and accepted story. That birds sing to attract their appointed mates and that lions roar to intimidate their foes, is quite understood. All of these things are in their own way beautiful, wonderful, purposeful. Colour and sound, then, in Nature are both put to utilitarian purposes; and we understand that these two, the bases of art and music, when found in natural objects, are there by reason of no accident, however happy; and yet, in the face of this, one occasionally runs across serious-minded persons, readers many and writers not a few, who have the temerity to question whether Nature has any especial intent when she adopts a given form for one of her productions. It is equivalent to saying that this same Nature which gives the milk-weed its colour for a purpose, nevertheless makes its flower five-pointed and always five-pointed by mere chance and without any design or intention: That the lily and the snow crystal, both drift white and symbolic to our mind of purity, receive their colour as part of a deep-laid plan, but that both are six-pointed, always six-pointed, and hexagonal in every detail, only because Nature has not thought to make them anything else,—a mere matter of negligent convenience on her part, without meaning or significance.

As for me, while I freely admit that in only a limited number of instances is it possible to say why Nature has ascribed selected forms to certain of her creations, yet I am entirely satisfied that when she gives to the white pine a sheaf of five leaves or needles and to the pitch pine only three, she is aiming at a definite result which she knows exactly how to achieve and with all of the confidence acquired through a million successes; a definite result so sure and satisfactory that, like the Almighty whom she represents, she shows "neither variableness nor shadow of turning."

May we not then concede that unless Nature can be said to have a definite purpose in her use of form and proportion in both animate and inanimate creation and that unless these factors have a direct bearing on the relations of beauty throughout the world, further pursuit of research along these lines is time misused? Once we recognise, however, that these forms and proportions are far from being accidental, and that they arise from a purpose, unknown perhaps but full of significance, then, along with colour and sound, their study in things natural will take on a new interest and become the substratum of an abundant research in beauty and art.

UNITS OF MEASUREMENT

It will be clear to the veriest beginner in such matters that no measurement of the forms and proportions of natural objects could be carried out were it dependent upon the use of standard units such as the inch, the foot, the centimeter, and the meter. Two other methods however lie open to us and they may both be used in harmony. By the first of these, we may gain all the information desired relative to the number of parts or items of a certain kind produced in each natural group, as we counted the five needles in the sheaf of white pine and the number of sides in a snow crystal. In this way we may determine whether Nature repeats the same number of factors in any completed production when she creates another of the same class. By the second mode, we can measure one part of any object under observation by the position or dimensions of another part, always bearing in mind that the relative shapes and forms, and not the sizes in inches are the points of comparison. By this mode we may compare the relative shapes, forms, proportions, angles and decorations of any two chosen specimens or types and again determine whether these various factors are among those which Nature repeats. In the end perhaps we shall understand something of the advantages which are derived by Nature in the use of certain proportional forms in her creations.

So long as we employ the first of the methods above and confine our mathematics to mere arithmetic, little need be said in amplification; but, because it is realised that a work of this kind, if it be of service, will necessarily fall continually into the hands of those whose need in life has not thrown them into the use of other branches of mathematics, the proofs employed here will be of the simplest possible kind, confining all demonstrations to such terms as can easily be defined, pausing occasionally for an explanation which may appear wholly unnecessary to those trained in mathematical lore and precision. The result will at times lack that brevity and crispness which the use of more advanced mathematical formulæ would produce, but which, unfortunately, would perhaps be as an unknown tongue to the very reader most interested in understanding the result. The second of the two modes of measurement referred to above, that of comparison and logical analysis of the spaces, lines, and angles composing the structure or decorations of an object, would come within the general subject of geometry and in order that those who have never thoroughly mastered this wonderful study may share in its beauties, such steps as are involved in the points described will be taken up and explained with all the brevity possible.

NUMERICAL UNITS

Before becoming too much involved in the processes of comparing Nature's various methods, even by the counting of completed parts, it will repay us to take the time to realise that even the numbers with which we shall work have certain fundamental characteristics, entirely divorced from the question of what specific thing is being numbered by their use; and in order to understand the chapters which follow, I shall, even at the expense of repetition, restate a few of the principles set out in *Nature's Harmonic Unity*. We shall find, then, that numbers, taken abstractly, bear certain harmonic relations to each other regardless of concrete objects. The number *one* for example, stands in a class by itself. Multiplied by itself, it produces itself ($1 \times 1 = 1$): divided by itself, it again reproduces itself ($1 \div 1 = 1$): the square, the cube and the Nth power of *one* are all *one* and their roots are constantly self-productive in the same way. The reciprocal of *one* is again *one*, and while *one* is the only exact divisor of all other integers, so also are all other integers its exact multiple. In this invariable reaction upon itself, it will be found like no other integer and in the estimation of the ancients the lowest number stood, as logically it must, for "position" only, since it could show only that, and neither direction, surface, nor content.

The number *two* on the contrary, being formed by the addition of *one* and *one*, may show not only position but direction or distance as well, having a fixed start and termination, while *three*, being capable of indicating not only a beginning and an ending but a middle as well, therefore represents the lowest integral form capable of indicating at the same time both length and breadth and outlining a plane surface; so *four* holds the factors necessary to the indication of a solid having length, breadth, and thickness. These four are the principal elements or fundamentals in the old Pythagorean system in which they are designated the "monad," the "duad," which proceeds from the union of "monad" and "monad," the "triad," proceeding from the union of monad and duad, and the "tetrad," produced by the union of duad and duad. These four integers are the only ones presenting characteristics requiring our examination, and we may therefore proceed to the consideration of numbers themselves in groups or series.

Taking a group of numbers together, we frequently find upon analysis, that they have certain interesting relations to each other. Suppose for example we see the numbers 2, 5, 8, 11, 14. A moment's thought shows us that these stand separated by intervals of three and that were they continued, there is a certain logic in assuming that the next number would be seventeen, and immediately we understand that a relation exists between these numbers which has characteristics strong enough to impress itself on the mind. There are a great many forms of such "progressions" or "series" but all, on analysis, have this power to suggest their own continuance and to indicate the next term. The one above, where the succeeding term is arrived at by a mere addition, comes under the grouping of an arithmetical progression, while such a series as 2, 4, 8, 16, 32, where the succession is extended by multiplication instead of addition, will be recognised as a geometrical progression. The intervals supplied by either addition or multiplication may, of course, be filled by any number whatsoever, and the variety is endless. In addition to these progressions we must notice another variety commonly called the "recurring series," in which the intervals, while not all equal as in the progressions, must, nevertheless, recur in the same order, as in the case of such a series as 2, 6, 8, 11, 13, 17, 19, 22, etc., in which the respective intervals are seen to be 4, 2, 3, 2, and then repeating 4, 2, 3, 2, again.

Our examination so far has been but a necessary preliminary to the comprehension of two most important facts if we are to undertake any examination of natural examples or forces; and this will be equally true whether our examination be carried on by mere numbering of parts or by geometrical comparison. In either case we must have the patience of pursue these dull explanations.

We have now arrived at the great point to be attained in thus examining numbers, for of all of the various forms of series, the most interesting by far is the one which we shall here take up. It will be observed that, given several of the factors of a series, the mind, in simple cases, supplies the rest intuitively, as would the eye if the series were one of spaces, or the ear if recurrent sounds were involved. There is thus a natural inclination of the mind to combine any two things under consideration, using the result as a new step or member, to be in turn combined again. Such a process naturally commences where all numeration begins, with the unit, and grows thus: $1 + 1 = 2$; $2 + 1 = 3$; $3 + 2 = 5$; $5 + 3 = 8$; $8 + 5 = 13$; $13 + 8 = 21$; $21 + 13 = 34$, etc., and thus continuing to combine each pair for the production of a new member. To those versed in such matters I need hardly introduce the well-known "Fibonacci Series." It is frequently stumbled upon in works on Nature and is extremely useful in the numbering of completed factors where a count is necessary, besides being the nearest integral equivalent to that Extreme and Mean proportion which we shall find flung broadcast throughout Nature. [1]

GEOMETRIC UNITS

In examining the various series coming under the section denoted "Numerical Units" we have recognised that these were naturally grouped into three great families, the arithmetical progressions, the geometrical progressions, and the recurring series. The use of such family groupings is of very great service, since it enables a mathematician to know the exact powers and relations which he may expect to find existing between the various members of a series the moment he learns to what group it belongs, nor need he complicate his work nor burden his mental spaces with further details. Both before and since collaborating on *Nature's Harmonic Unity* I

[1] *Nature's Harmonic Unity*, Appendix, and Appendix, Note XXIV post.

have spent a great deal of time in studying the proportions exhibited in the processes of Nature and in applying to these and to adaptations of them in art, the accurate solvent of mathematics and logic. The more I have delved into the mathematical phenomena and the natural and scientific examples constantly coming to hand, the more it is borne in upon me that by eliminating many of the comparatively unimportant factors and allowing the balance to group themselves along natural family lines into which research proves that they naturally fall, the matter might be put into forms much simplified, forms so simple as to be open to every serious student and yet placed upon a basis so accurate as to defy contradiction.

A brief and crude explanation of a portion of what I have in mind may be taken from everyday life. If we wish to convey the information that certain friends of ours have taken a cottage at the seaside, it is only necessary to state that the Johnsons have rented a cottage at the beach. How very complex it would be were it required that instead of this we should inform our hearer that Harry Johnson, with Amelia Johnson (née Brown) to whom he was married ten years ago last Easter, together with his four children Margaret, Lucy, Charles, and Jack, aged respectively seven, five, three, and one, and being all blonds like their mother and chubby like their father, were going to the cottage at the beach with their uncle Jack, for whom the little boy was named, accompanied by their various trunks and dolls, paraphernalia and impedimenta, to spend the summer. Progress through life would be not only slow but dull with such hindrances, and almost unconsciously we accept the habit and benefit of using types to indicate groups in matters of information, thus saving the need of repeating endless chains of detail, which are absolutely necessary but which, once the family group be ascertained, may safely be inferred rather than repeated.

In exactly the same way, I would divide the necessary mathematical and natural examples into those groups into which they logically fall and which will furnish us with the greatest number of constantly recurring examples. We have seen how the use of family groupings, as accepted by mathematicians in the field of numerical series, simplifies matters to which they apply. In the same way, analysis shows that natural groups exist in the geometrical unit families, and that of these, three stand out as so much more prominent and of so much more frequent occurrence than the others, that for the moment the rest may be held negligible; and as families, we will consider only these three: the four-sided group, which I have designated the Tetragon Family, the Family of Extreme and Mean Proportion, and that variable group in which the focal position and the radial length, or both, constantly vary, and which group may be designated as the Asymmetrical Family. These three, with their subdivisions, are three of *Nature's Great Modules*, and later examinations will disclose that these families are not merely geometric, but that Nature herself groups her works in the same way, and frequently along the same lines of demarkation.

THE TETRAGON FAMILY

The first of these families to be examined will be the group which geometrically covers the square, the octagon, which is its nearest relative, the equilateral triangle (a first cousin) and the hexagon (a first cousin once removed). These form a great family which governs vast forms of energy and are manifested as we shall see in gravitation, vibratory forces such as light and sound, come constantly into evidence in astronomy, are recurrent very persistently in all demonstrations of polar force, and are, generically speaking, always to be found wherever kinetic energy produces motion, or molecular action shows its effects. This group is taken up first in order both because of its importance, which is great, and for the comparative simplicity which surrounds the demonstrations.

Once it is shown how these various members of the same family hang together, it will be realised that, having in any one instance demonstrated that the group governs a proposition, it need not be required that all of the separate steps and correlations be gone into again. Once put clearly into diagrammatic shape, we shall be able to understand that as surely as Smith's son is Smith in turn, so surely will further coincidences of the same kind develop a second time and these need be shown but once. This will greatly serve to simplify all of the work both of argument, drawing, and proof and save endless and tedious repetition.

In order to illustrate what I have in mind, it will be seen that in plate 1 I have set out, in accordance with geometric principles often utilised in science, an ordinary progression of the square and octagon in the same prime circle, and the diagram is so simple as almost to explain itself. Within this circle designated as "prime" we shall inscribe a square. Again within the square and tangent to its sides, a second circle, inside which another square is drawn. This process can, of course, be carried on *ad infinitum*, but the two progressions described will serve for the illustration. This process of geometrical comparison is very old and no claim is laid to originality in its construction. Any book on engineering which contains the customary tables will, moreover, demonstrate that octagons, inscribed in the various circles, will exactly coincide with the corners of the square; that the position of the second square in the progression (marked "C") divides the radius of the prime square (AO) into exact halves, and that if a circle be drawn within this square with the radius CO it will be precisely "octant" to the prime circle. Also we shall learn by the same process that the radius AO is the exact measure of the side IJ (second square) and so we know that the new radius in turn will be the side of the next ensuing or third square should one be drawn, as at MN. Also it is very interesting to note that each diagonal equals the next preceding side, thus IL equals EF and MQ equals IJ. Thus it is plain that these squares and octagons, measured by inscribed circles, form, by a sort of law of primogeniture, the direct line of the Tetragon Family by descent, and for the purposes of a further study, the exact relations of these progressing squares and octagons have been expressed in percentages of the prime radius and set down in the appendix for reference.[1]

Having the coincidences indicated in plate 1 well in mind, let us now turn for a moment to plate 2 in which we shall find the proportions relative to another branch of the same family, and a brief examination will prove that the two are as truly members of the same family as two brothers or cousins. And this, interesting to relate, is not merely true in geometry, as I have said, but demonstration shows that Nature, not satisfied merely to accept the geometrical similarity between the square and the trigon or equilateral triangle as illustrated in the diagram, goes on to connect the two even in her rules and laws as we shall see in the chapter on force.

Inspection of plate 2 will confirm this idea that the tetragon and the trigon are first cousins, and they eternally hunt in couples. Wherever you find the one, the other is lurking in the background

[1] Appendix, Note I.

just around the corner. They are practically inseparable.   Let us
then, take a prime circle of the same size as before, and, inserting

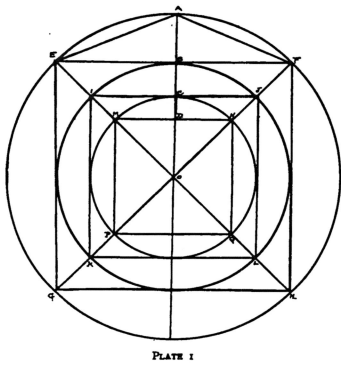

PLATE I

TETRAGON FAMILY

or inscribing in it an equilateral triangle ATV, we begin to find the
traces of this family relation at once, particularly when we add the
inscribed hexagon which is next of kin to the equilateral triangle
in the same way that the octagon is obviously descended from the

square as seen in plate 1. You will remember that in the first illustration we saw that the radius AO of the prime circle was the same.

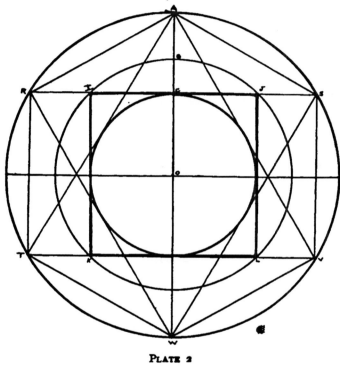

PLATE 2
HEXAGON GROUP

length as the side of the square IJ of the second progression, and looking at plate 2 we find (as sustained by the absolutely accurate mathematical analysis in the appendix[17]) that this same radius AO which, in the first instance, measures the side of the second square as well as measuring the prime circumference, when put into its relation with the equilateral triangle and the hexagon, measures with absolute perfection the side of the hexagon also. By this coincidence, the length of the hexagon (RA), the radius of the prime circle (AO), the side of the second square (IJ), and the diagonal of the third square (MQ) are all identical.[1]

Beginning again, we found on our original experiment that the upper side of the second square as first inscribed was placed at a point exactly half way from the circumference of the prime circle to the centre; now, in plate 2 we find that the upper side of the inscribed equilateral triangle is precisely so placed and cuts the radius AO in the same halves at the point C. Thus we have the side of the hexagon, the radius of the prime circle and the side of the square of the second progression and the diagonal of the third square all of the same length, while the side of the triangle coincides absolutely with the position of the side of the second square. And these coincidences can be multiplied indefinitely.[1] Surely the most amicable of cousins could scarcely agree better nor more clearly show their blood relationship.

The demonstrations have, however, been so far confined to those in plane surfaces and requiring only two dimensions, being in fact the simplest form except those merely linear. In order to

Appendix, Notes II and III.

test the plan we have in mind it will be necessary to go further into the matter and consider for a moment whether or no these same principles of comparative measurement and proportion can be

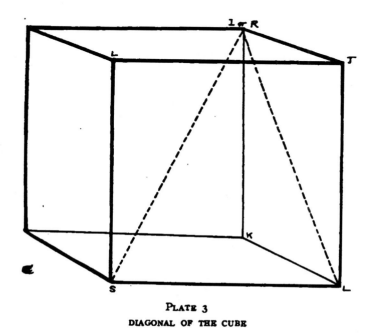

PLATE 3

DIAGONAL OF THE CUBE

applied to solids and for illustrative purposes will turn to plate 3 where the solid selected is the commonest of all, the cube or four-figured rectangular solid.

In making comparative measurements of surfaces and of solids it is, for many purposes, convenient to compare them by their diagonals, not alone because the diagonal determines both the point of beginning of the base and that terminating the vertical sides as well, but also because the diagonal is the index of the area. Taking this convenient means of comparison, let us apply it to the solid in question, and in order that the result may be both simple and accurate, let us assume that the sides of our cube are formed of squares (I, J, K, L) of the same proportions as the same square in plates 1 and 2. Then the diameter of the surface shown in the square I, J, K, L will be the diagonal I, L and in plate 3 this will correspond with the same diagonal in plates 1 and 2 and the coincidences there noted will again occur. In order however to get at the diagonal factor of the cube itself, we must conceive a line as drawn from the lower left-hand front corner of the cube as marked S, through the solid and emerging at the upper-right back corner, marked R (or I). Starting thus with a cube based on squares identical with the square I, J, K, L in the previous diagrams, and having the diagonal IL on the surface, it is not a little astonishing to find that the diagonal of the cube as a solid (RS) measures, by trigonometrical solution, precisely the same as the side of the first progression of the equilateral triangle.[1]

Thus as between the progressing squares, octagons, triangles, hexagons, and cubes, drawn on the same identical unit of base as

[1] Appendix, Note IV.
It is essential of course to recollect that the mere measurement on paper in plate 3 will not produce this result since it is drawn in perspective. The result however is absolutely correct.

shown, we find the following really noteworthy coincidences, amongst many others which have not been listed here:

(A) These are all absolutely equal in length:
  (1) Radius of the prime circle:
  (2) Side of the second square
  (3) The side of the hexagon
  (4) Diagonal of the side of the cube

(B) These are also equal in length:
  (5) Side of the equilateral triangle
  (6) Diagonal of the solid cube

(C) These are coincident in position, as measured from the centre of the prime circle:
  (7) Side of the second square
  (8) Ends of the hexagon
  (9) Side of the equilateral triangle

Let us then, since these coincidences can, as ascertained and described, be carried out indefinitely and quite beyond patience, agree that we may feel at liberty not only to let these examples suffice, but in future safely to rest content that, whenever we cross evidences of the Tetragon Family in any one of its branches, the remainder may be assumed as sure to follow without going separately each time into all of the many ramifications. The innumerable cases in which we shall require the use of these principles necessitates that the simplest form be adopted, and the later chapters will be devoted to demonstrations of their usefulness and of the frequency with which they occur in Nature, science, and art.

I have said before that the three families so constantly referred to were not merely geometric, but that Nature herself groups her works in the same way and along the same lines of demarkation. For the present purpose, it is sufficient with regard to the Tetragon Family to show geometrically that there is a constant falling together of the members of the clan as I have described them, leaving Nature's applications, not merely of the geometrical principle but of the family groupings, to later pages. As illustrative, however, of the persistence with which the members of the Tetragon Family indicate one another, I might in passing call attention to the two solids which belong to the simple and less intricate end of this group —to wit the solid bounded by equilateral triangles called the tetrahedron, and the cube or hexahedron, bounded by squares. The one having four faces with three sides each, and the other having six faces of four sides and angles. A four-sided figure (tetrahedron) with three-sided faces, and a six-sided figure (hexahedron) with four-sided faces. How intimately each calls the other to mind, and how veritably each typifies the subtle relations of all of the members of this intimate family.

THE PENTAGON FAMILY

This family or group is of importance equal to the one just examined and has from time immemorial served to interest students under the designation of THE GOLDEN SECTION. That time-honoured mathematical formula to which the ancients gave the name "Divine Ratio," engaged the attention of Euclid and the thoughts of countless mathematicians since, being generally referred to as the Extreme and Mean Proportion; and concerning this a somewhat exhaustive analysis was presented to the readers of *Nature's Harmonic Unity*. The relation between this extreme and mean proportion as a series and all forms of the pentagon is a matter of the greatest interest, and whether it ever came to the knowledge of the ancient investigators or not, it can now be made clear beyond peradventure of a doubt, placing these two constantly recurring forms in an interrelation that is indisputable. [1]

That numbers have certain interesting relations to each other I have endeavoured to explain, and in writing on the correlations of numbers, the nature and relations of this ratio have already been

[1] Appendix Notes to *Nature's Harmonic Unity*, pages 289, 290, Notes 7 and 11, and conclusively on page 299.

touched upon. Owing to the frequency of the references made to it hereafter, a few moments spent by the reader now in understanding its peculiarities will simplify many of the statements to be met in the coming pages.

Let it be constantly carried in mind that the expressions "extreme and mean proportion" and "a mean proportional between two other terms" are very far from being synonymous. The peculiar ratio under examination is in general but rudely understood and must be somewhat further explained. We must in the first place remember that presumably Pythagoras had a clear grasp of the subject, although of course the Egyptians and ancient Greeks were hampered in their use of such proportions by their lack of knowledge concerning fractions. To them the geometric proposition, represented by easily divided lines, was clearly comprehensible, while numerically their knowledge was restricted in all such matters to such use as could be made of integral approximates in place of decimal perfection.

Well-known formula in mathematics have a habit of taking to themselves, as time goes on, designations whereby they may be indicated briefly. Ot this kind is the use of the Greek letter "pi" (π) now universally indicating the relation of the diameter to its circumference in the arithmetical decimal of .31415927 for which it is constantly substituted. In the writing of *Nature's Harmonic Unity*, where the almost unlimited influence of the continuing series of extreme and mean proportion as developed in the analysis was one of the oft-touched themes, and where the desire to impress upon the reader the importance of this series which was there called a "measuring rod flung broadcast throughout all Nature," the need was repeatedly felt for some designation less clumsy than the expression "perfect and continuing series of extreme and mean proportion," however accurate and descriptive that expression undoubtedly was. Since the publication of the former work other writers in speaking of this series as set out, have doubtless felt the same need; and one, at least, has partly bridged the chasm by designating our series by the Greek letter *phi* (φ), a designation which I am loath even temporarily to abandon, both because it has points of argument in its favour and because it has been presented by men whose names carry weight. In spite of this, certain objections inhere in the name "phi" as suggested and because of these, which are specified in the appendix, it has been thought best to adhere to the one which we had coined originally for the former work. The division of a line into extreme and mean ratio has been known since the day of Euclid as the Golden Section. Why not, therefore, most appropriately, consider this indefinitely continuous series, growing out of the same ratio, as the "Golden Series." This seems so reasonable, so logical, so simple and free from objection that, in spite of the desire to conform to every suggestion where possible, the use of the name Golden Series in this relation has been perpetuated in the present work in preference to any other so far in view.[1]

The best definition of this ratio which I have been able to construct is the one used in the former work, and here repeated:

By the expression extreme and mean proportion is meant *the division of a quantity into two such parts or proportions as that the measure of the whole quantity shall bear the same relation to the measure of the greater part as the measure of the greater part bears in turn to the measure of the lesser;* or, changing the form without altering the effect, we may with equal truth say that *of two separate quantities, the lesser must be to the greater as the greater is to their sum.*

A moment's consideration will show the difference between this and any other form of proportion, since in all others any one of the terms may be varied, producing a corresponding variation in its opposing member. There is, on the contrary (barring of course the use of negative signs), but one form of extreme and mean proportion, since the last term is fixed, being the sum of the other two. We may say, for instance, that 2 : 4 :: 4 : 8 or 2 : 5 :: 5 : 10, and in both cases the one term is a mean proportional between the other two, yet in neither case is there even an approximation to the extreme and mean proportion. In other words, in the extreme and mean proportion, as

[1] *See* Appendix, Note V.

the sum cannot be varied, neither of the other two members may be changed and still remain proportional to the whole.

Thus it will be clear that while the variety of forms in which a mean proportional may be expressed is limited only by the ingenuity and patience of the student in their construction, on the other hand there is one and only one form of an exact extreme and mean proportion, barring, as I have already said, the use of negative terms and signs. By the introduction of negative signs, however, only the details are changed and not the generic facts, and no prolonged reference will be made to combinations deduced through the interpolation of negative signs since only confusion would result on the part of those to whom these intricacies are unfamiliar, while, on the other hand, those who understand such details are perfectly competent to apply the substantial facts here set forth to the new conditions resultant from the negative combination.

Since the uses to which we shall put this proportion will not be purely academic, it may not be amiss to understand it geometrically as well as numerically. Looking now at plate 4, diagram A, if we consider the line AB to be so divided at the point C as that CB : AC :: AC : AB, then the entire quantity AB will be divided into extreme and mean proportion, and this will be demonstrably invariable since the sum AB cannot be increased or diminished to correspond with any change produced in the other terms by the movement of the point C.

We shall find later in these notes that the decimal or percentage equivalent of extreme and mean ratio is almost indispensable to the work, and in order to make both the geometrical relation and this numerical index clear I take the liberty of submitting the same Euclidean demonstration of the proportion in question that was used some years ago in the previous work, showing with great clearness how this division may be accomplished, following which the study of the numerical equivalent can be readily pursued.

We are now in position to return to our own lines in determining what may be the decimal value or equivalent of the extreme and mean proportion. Turning again to the plate, let us give to the line AB the hypothetical value of one hundred units. Then, as the line BF is half of AB it will equal fifty units and $\overline{AF}^2 = \overline{AB}^2 + \overline{BF}^2$ or by substituting units, $\overline{AF}^2 = 12,500$ or AF = $\sqrt{12,500}$ or 111.803399, and since AD = AF − DF, we have AD = 111.803399 − 50. = 61.803399, as already shown in the appendix to the former work.

It therefore follows that when two quantities are respectively .38196601 and .61803399 of each whole unit of their sum, *then and only then*, they will bear to each other the relation of an extreme and mean proportion, except as this truth may be extended by the use of negatives, and this expresses their absolutely accurate percentage of the sum.

This matter of the decimal value of extreme and mean ratio has

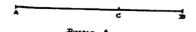

Diagram A

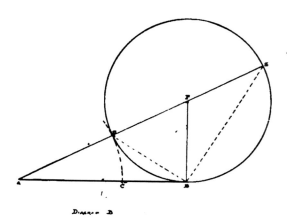

Diagram B

PLATE 4

EXTREME AND MEAN RATIO

(From Nature's Harmonic Unity)

Examining Plate 4, Diagram B, we find a method of division into extreme and mean proportion which is as old as Christianity, and for which I naturally make no claim to originality. It has, however, the merit of being perfectly clear, though rudimentary.

Let the line AB be any given quantity. Erect a perpendicular, as BF, from one end, as at B, equal to one half of the line AB. Then with F as a centre and radius BF, describe a circle and connect the points A and E. On the line AB lay off AC equal to AD, then will the point C divide the line AB into extreme and mean proportion, for

In the triangles ABD and EAB the angle A is common, and ABD, formed by a tangent and chord, is measured by one half of the angle BD which also measures the angle E at the circumference. The two triangles are therefore similar and their sides are proportional, hence AE : AB : : AB : AD and by division AE − AB : AB :: AB − AD : AD.

Since, however, radius equals one half of AB, the diameter, or DE, will equal AB and consequently AE − AB equals AD or its equivalent AC. Since AC equals AD it follows that AB − AD equals AB − AC or CB. Substituting these values for the terms of the equation we have AC : AB :: CB : AC or by inversion, CB : AC :: AC : AB, thus proving that the point C divides the quantity AB into an extreme and mean proportion.

3

been taken up at some length because, in a long investigation of kindred subjects and the scientific workings of this peculiar proportion, I have found numberless instances where a definite formula of expression was absolutely requisite, which should be sufficiently flexible to denote extreme and mean proportion with equal facility, whether as a linear, superficial, bulk, or spherical measure, and of the several forms possible, the decimal equivalent presents the only basis of comparison suited to a work of this kind.

It has frequently been stated that for purposes of design the continuing series known as the Fibonacci Ratio of 3; 5; 8; 13 formed a perfect basis. As this series, however, does not form a perfect constant in the usual sense, I am again introducing the serial factors as they were presented in *Nature's Harmonic Unity*, so that no misapprehension may occur; and, to call attention to the actual conditions, a tabulation showing just what is the relation between this series and a true proportion, is here repeated from the previous work. No reference to the limiting ratio or summation of the Fibonacci series is here made, both because it is too involved and because no use is made of it.

It will be here noticed that when the perfect ratio has reached the point of 34 : 55 it is approximately the same as the decimal .61803399 of extreme and mean proportion, though this does not hold good for the Fibonacci series, thus again emphasising the superiority of the divine section.

Fibonacci Series (imperfect ratios)	Perfect ratios (not extreme and mean)	Decimal ratios (not Fibonacci)
1 : 2 :: 2 : 3	1 : 2 :: 2 : 4	.50
2 : 3 :: 3 : 5	2 : 3 :: 3 : 4.5	.6666
3 : 5 :: 5 : 8	3 : 5 :: 5 : 8.3333	.60
5 : 8 :: 8 : 13	5 : 8 :: 8 : 12.80	.625
8 : 13 :: 13 : 21	8 : 13 :: 13 : 21.125	.615
13 : 21 :: 21 : 34	13 : 21 :: 21 : 33.92	.6190
21 : 34 :: 34 : 55	21 : 34 :: 34 : 55.04	.6176
34 : 55 :: 55 : 89	34 : 55 :: 55 : 88.97	.6181

It being thus made clear that, when treated either continuously or as an exact proportion, the Fibonacci series contains imperfections, it is appropriate to examine further and see if the same defects inhere in the extreme and mean ratio. Whether we test this proportion arithmetically or algebraically, we shall immediately find that it presents all of the possibilities of a perfect, continuing series.

Referring to our definition, we see that if, of two quantities, the less is to the greater as the greater is to their sum, or if $y : x :: x : y + x$, then the terms are in extreme and mean proportion, and may be solved by the Euclidean formula, $x^2 = y^2 + xy$ which we may express in the words "the square of the greater equals the square of the lesser added to the rectangle of the two." If, now, this proportion is a true continuing series, then the following will be true:

$$(1)\ x : x+y :: x + y : 2x+y,$$

and in serial form,

$$(2)\ y : x :: x + y : 2x+y,\ \text{etc.}$$

Transforming both of these into their equations, we have the Euclidean formula above as a result in each case, and hence we may again add these important generalisations; that *in every extreme and mean proportion, the greater is to the sum as the sum is to the greater plus the sum; the less is to the greater as the sum is to the greater plus the sum; that these two conditions continue indefinitely; and that the true extreme and mean proportion is a perfect continuing series.*

Illustrated arithmetically we find, by the decimal equivalent, that

$$.38196601 : .61803399 :: 1.0000: 1.61803399\ [1]$$

which of course is clearly a perfect proportion since its solution gives us .61803399 on both sides.

It is perhaps almost unnecessary to say again in this work that the same ratio may be carried out descending, whereby is obtained a series consisting of the square, cube, fourth power, etc., of the decimal equivalent of the greater of the two terms, thus:

[1] *Nature's Harmonic Unity*, Appendix, Note page 287 and Appendix, Note, V^b post.

$1 : .61803399 \ (x) : .38196601 \ (x^2) : .2360673 \ (x^3) : .145902 \ (x^4) :$
$.090170 \ (x^5) : .055728 \ (x^6) : .0344417 \ (x^7) : .0212863 \ (x^8),$ etc.[1]

The information thus gathered will be sufficient for the purpose at hand in so far as the extreme and mean proportion is treated as a linear or superficial measure. We shall, however, have occasion to consider this series as an angular measure, and a moment must shortly be given to its examination from this standpoint.

Pursuing further then, the relation of this extreme and mean proportion to the pentagon and pentagram, as has been done in our previous work and must necessarily be undertaken to some extent here, I would first state in brief what I mean by the pentagram as the term is one of only occasional use.

The pentagon or five-sided regular polygon yields the pentagram or five-pointed star by the joining of its opposite angles. The pentagram, otherwise known as the pentacle, is described by a well-known authority as "A mathematical figure used in magical ceremonies and considered a defence against demons. It was probably with this figure that the Pythagoreans began their letters as a symbol of health. In many modern English books, it is assumed that this is the six-pointed star formed of two triangles interlaced or superimposed as in Solomon's seal. Obviously the pentacle *must* be a five-pointed star

[1] *Nature's Harmonic Unity*, Appendix, Note, page 287.

or a five-membered object, as equivalent to the pentagram or pentalpha. The construction of the five-pointed star depends upon an abstruse proposition discovered by the Pythagorean school and this star seems to have been from that time adopted as their seal." Another eminent authority refers to this figure as being "the triple interwoven triangle or pentagram—star-shaped *pentagon*—used as a symbol or sign of recognition by the Pythagoreans."

As the theories of the Pythagoreans would apply perfectly to the pentagonal form and hardly at all to the six-pointed one, and as both history and etymology sustain the five-pointed figure, I submit as an explanation of the difference of opinion, the reconciling statement that both forms can be originated by the use of interlaced triangles,—the six-pointed star by using two equilateral triangles, and the five-pointed one by the use of three isosceles triangles. This fact seems to have escaped the attention of many observers, who have concluded that only the six-pointed star could be created from the trigon, and have by this been led into calling the hexagonal outline a pentagram,—an evident misnomer.

Having obtained a decimal index of extreme and mean proportion in a preceding paragraph, one of the first striking features in the examination of the pentagon will be the persistence with which it presents this ratio; and that, not in a mere approximation, but in the absolutely true and precise sense. A number of instances in which this occurs in both the pentagram and the pentagon proper will be mentioned as they are reached, but the fact should be kept in mind constantly in the examination.

Having now a fair working idea of what constitutes extreme and mean proportion as a continuous and unending golden series and having shown how it may be applied both to linear and numerical measurements, it should be observed that it is an error and a great deprivation to consider this mystic series from one standpoint to the· exclusion of all others.   To view it only as a means of subdividing a line is to subvert its meaning, since we are no more justified in restricting this great series to use in measuring mere lines than we are to chain our conception of physical things to a fantastic country having length and breadth but no thickness; for the bearing of extreme and mean proportion can be shown to have as direct a relation on all dimensions and methods of computation as it has upon mere distances or enumeration.   This primal fact I take pains to emphasise for the reason that it has escaped the examination of so many writers on the subject, this absorbingly interesting ratio being almost universally treated as a mathematical toy and a curiosity rather than as a module continually occurring in Nature and science, not to mention art; and a module as demonstrably applicable to superficial areas, curves, angles, and solids as it is to the simpler matters to which it has generally been applied, when applied at all.   Before going into values other than the linear and numerical, as touched by this proportion, as a mere matter of precaution I would briefly repeat, however, that when considered algebraically, this measure, like all others, is subject to treatment under the negative sign. After all, a series of demonstrations in negatives would, perhaps, add to the interest of the student but would surely add nothing to the truth.

We have started out with a brief explanation of the numerical or arithmetical form of this series, which applies naturally and directly to all linear measurements, and the first of the additional matters to be considered would seem logically to be the measurement of superficial spaces, or areas as expressed in planes. The superficial value of a plane cannot be said to be the mere combined linear values of its bounding sides themselves. A plane rectangle bounded by sides respectively five and eight units in length could hardly be rated at a comparative of thirteen, since that is the linear sum and not the co-operative value or potential of the factors, which in reality produce a plane of five times eight or forty units as its total measure. The index of such a plane would be, rather the diagonal which connects its opposite angles than the sum of the component sides. This diagonal, requiring both direction and distance in its location, forms a graph of the terms of the plane as shown in the tetragon solid, and brings into the problem the two factors necessary to constitute surface by the expression of the dimensions both of length and breadth.

In creating, then, a golden plane in extreme and mean proportion, we shall have the sides formed by lines representing the lesser and the greater terms: and in such a plane we shall find that the diagonal index measures 1.175571 in percentage of the greater side, whatever that may be, and that the angle at the base is 58° 16′ 57″.[1] Thus in plate 5 the plane ABCO is formed by the lines the length of which are in extreme and mean proportion, thus, AO : AB :: AB : AO + AB and the line BO will equal 1.175571 of AB, a point of which we shall see the importance a little later.

The value of the module should not stop, however, with its ability to admeasure plane surfaces, nor does the extreme and mean proportion fail of further interest.   Let us create a solid, bounded by planes in regular golden progression.   Two of these bounding planes will then be formed by lines bearing to each other the relation of the lesser to the greater in an extreme and mean ratio, and two other sides will be bounded by planes formed of lines the shorter of which will be the original greater term while the longer will be equal to the sum of the original less and the original greater, being itself thus the next progressive term in our extreme and mean progression when treated as a perfect and continuing series.   In such a solid, symbolic of extreme and mean ratio, and formed out of the factors constituting its progression, we shall again use the diagonal as our index, and the result-

[1] Appendix, Note VI.

ant coincidences are not a little remarkable when compared with those which have gone before and will follow. In this phi solid, formed of the exact factors of the series, we shall find disclosed these illuminating comparisons:

In a logical solid as formed in plate 6 we have as a base the line CO (phi x), as a verticle, BC (phi x′) and for the length, the line OD (phi x″) all being in continuing proportion. The verticle plane ABCO is then the same as the basic plane ABCO in plate 5, merely being seen here in perspective. The diagonal of this plane (BO) bears, therefore, the same relation to the sides AB, BC, as in the plate referred to and is 1.175571 of the length of the greater side BC.

In this solid of extreme and mean proportion, we have

(A)   The edges of the planes in extreme and mean ratio,

(B)   The lesser, AB, having a unit value of .38196601;

(C)   The greater, BC, having a value of .61803399 units;

(D)   The length being the sum, of a unit value of 1.00;

(E)   The diagonal of the plane (as AO) having the unit value of 1.175571;

(F)   The diagonal of the solid (as DB) will be of the unit value of 2.00;

(G)   The diagonal of the plane (BO) will form an angle of 58° 16′ 57″, while

(H) The diagonal of the solid (DB) will form with the side, the exact angle of the pentagon, 54° as measured from the perpendicular at vertex. ∠⌐⌐⌐

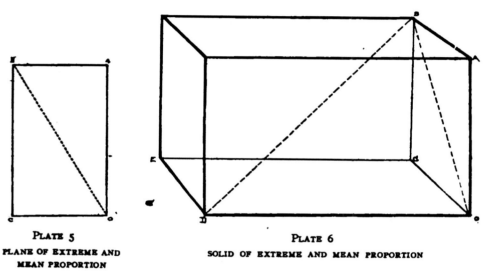

PLATE 5
PLANE OF EXTREME AND MEAN PROPORTION

PLATE 6
SOLID OF EXTREME AND MEAN PROPORTION

To those who are interested in the study of abstruse subjects, the examination of hyperspace questions, dealing with the so-called "Fourth Dimension," always appeal. Ordinary mortals cannot conceive an infinite world in which there should be either no dimensions at all on the one hand, or a fourth dimension, over and beyond the usual length, breadth, and thickness upon which we have been brought up. Is this fourth dimension a region of invisibility where souls play at large? Whatever we may think of it personally it is a recognised factor known and studied by mathematicians and scientists and it is susceptable of limited demonstration. In the same sense that the quadratic equation is the measure of all plane surfaces and the cubic equation measures all solids, so the tetradic equation, which presents no difficulties in mathematics, has been conceived to be the natural measure or index of the impractical and non-geometric figure constructed out of length, breadth, thickness, and the unknowable fourth dimension which is neither of these, and which, while we cannot comprehend it and cannot even prove that it exists, nevertheless yields to certain scientific and mathematical demonstrations and is a serviceable weapon along many scientific lines. It has indeed been used by a strange analogy in many metaphysical problems to produce solutions, some weird, and some, doubtless sound. It is not my purpose here to go farther into the question than simply to present it for the consideration of those who are interested and so to present it in connection with the great principle of extreme and mean proportion which we shall find underlying so many situations.[1]

It remains now to show in what manner the golden series can be applied to circular measurements before we go directly into the examination of specific cases where this progression exists.

In the mathematical notes to *Nature's Harmonic Unity*, I explained at some length what the circular or angular equivalent of

[1] For more extended discussion of the Fourth Dimensions, *see* Appendix, Note VII.

extreme and mean proportion consisted of and how this had been
arrived at, and it will perhaps be unnecessary here to go into great
length on the subject.   Plate 7 has been prepared for the purpose of
visualising what this circular equivalent
of the series looks like, and may be
explained thus.   Applying the decimal
equivalent of the two quantities constituting a perfect extreme and mean
proportion to the three hundred and
sixty degrees into which the circle is for
convenience arbitrarily divided, and
utilising the natural formula of
.38196601 : .61803399 :: x : 360°,   and
we have as a resultant circular equiva-

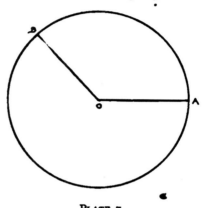

PLATE 7

ANGULAR EXTREME AND MEAN PROPOR-
TION

lent, 137° 30′ 27.954″ as being the less angle, while 222° 29′ 32.046″
represents the greater.   For the moment we shall rest content
with this achievement, taking up the application later in the
chapter.   (Appendix, Note V⁰.)

The obtuse angle AOB is the lesser of the two terms and
the balance of the circumference is measured by the comple-
mentary obtuse angle AOB.   In these two, the lesser is to the
greater as the greater is to the sum, or the entire circumference
of 360°.

PROMINENT MEMBERS OF THE PENTAGON GROUP

Now that we have examined the characteristics peculiar to this family as a whole, we are prepared to become better acquainted with several of the members individually, and the present sub-chapter will serve as a geometrical "Who's Who" in this Family. That all quantities and lines formed in golden proportions belong to the family is as obvious as that all plane and solid figures deliberately constructed in these terms are consistent members in good standing; but there are other geometrical forms and familiar quantities which come equally, though not so obviously, within its bounds. Of all recognised geometrical equilaterals, none so persistently, thoroughly, and undeviatingly yield evidences of extreme and mean proportion at every examination as the pentagon. This figure is really the tribal chief of all visible and familiar members of the clan and the more inquisitively one studies its various members, sides, diagonals, and intersections, the more one is assured that the whole structure of the pentagon is articulated upon a mathematically perfect system of extreme and mean proportion.

To show, now, how close is the relation between the pentagon, the pentagram, and this Divine Section in extreme and mean proportion, let us repeat some of the examinations previously made to that end.

Proceeding then without technicalities, let us, in plates 8 and 9, draw a perfect pentagon with its intersecting diagonals which form the beautiful figure of the pentagram or five-pointed star.   If we were to

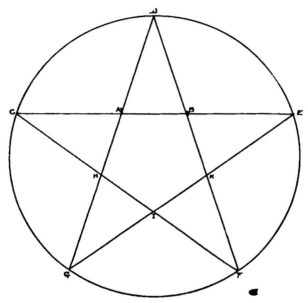

PLATE 8

THE PENTAGRAM.   PERFECT EXTREME AND MEAN PROPORTION

subject all of the subdivisions of the figure to the most rigid analytical test we should find extreme and mean ratios staring us in the face from every calculation.   For example, the sides of the perimeter, CD, DE, as shown in plate 9, etc., each bear the ratio in question to the respective diagonals DG, CF, etc., while the subdivisions AC,

AD, BE, etc., again bear the same relation to the sides of the peri-meter, which in this latter case become the greater form in the equation, where formally they were the less.   Again, the next smaller subdivisions of the pentagram, AB, BK, KI, IH, and HA which in turn form a second pentagon, with the apex turned downward, are in turn lesser terms of golden ratios in which lines leading to the outer points of the star, AD, DB, BE, EK, etc., may interchangeably be used as the greater factors.   Indeed the entire figure, taken in regular order, produces exactly that continuing series in the proportion of which we spoke a few pages previously and which might be expressed as AB : BE : DE : EG : x.   The number of coincidences to be noted is entirely beyond my patience to set forth or yours to read. I will, however, note a few golden proportions which are absolutely accurate (as all pentagonal—ratios are) and the reader may easily pick out numberless other combinations.

  (1)   AB: BE:: BE : AB+BE or AE

  (2)   BE: BC:: BC : BC+BE or CE

  (3)   DC : CE :: CE : CEF

  (4)   Twice the perimeter of the interior pentagon ABKIH is to the perimeter of the star, ADBEKFI, etc., as the latter is to twice the perimeter of the exterior pentagon CDE, etc.

  All of these are absolutely perfect extreme and mean proportions.[1]

---

[1] Appendix, Note VIII.

One may sum up the situation in the figure before us by saying that there are no unequal terms to be found which are not in this ratio to each other as forming a step in a perfect and continuing golden series.

This being so of the pentagon and the pentagram, let us go a step farther and judge the results of subjecting the pentagon to a form of progression such as was applied to the square and the equilateral triangle, and hinted at in plate 8. In the case of the pentagon, time will be saved by bowing to the overpowering evidence of the golden proportion in this figure, and we will draw plate 9 on this basis with a deliberate simplicity, by inscribing a pentagon within a circle and laying off the radius into a continued proportion, so that the outer end shall be to the inner end, as the latter is to the whole. Thus on the plate we shall have the radius which connects T and LP divided so that DL is to LT as LT is to DT, and the division will consequently be in this ratio. At L we shall draw another circle and in it inscribe a pentagon, and at the point M (same ratio between L and T) a third circle and a pentagon will be created: and if we examine these pentagons we shall find that not only do they bear the internal evidence of extreme and mean proportion with which they severally started as shown on plate 9, but that in addition, the sides of the star in the prime pentagon (AD for example) are exactly equal to the sides of the pentagon in the second progression (LN for instance) and hence another interminable series of perfect extreme and mean proportions is created such as AB : LN : : LN : CD (the sum of AB and NL). Looking again we find still farther evidence of a marked unity in this progression, since, with the second and third circles dividing the radius into extreme and mean proportion, the third pentagon coincides absolutely, both in position, distance from the centre, and length of sides, with the sides of the pentagon formed by the crossing of the pentagram in the prime figure as shown in plate 8.

If all of this is not enough, then let us go back a moment to plates 5 and 6 where you will recollect we jotted down some of the items relative to the logical solid. Among these you will note that we said that the diagonal of the golden plane (a rectangle bounded by lines in extreme and mean proportion) was 1.175571 times the greater side of the rectangle, and upon trigonometric calculation we find that this is exactly the relation of the radius TD if drawn would leave to the side of the pentagon CD, as well as of the radii TL and TM to the sides LN and AB. Again as the radius TD is exactly twice the perpendicular distance of the second pentagon from the centre, so the diagonal of the solid is exactly twice the length of the greater side, and once more the angle formed by the diagonal of the logical solid (54°) is exactly that which measures the pentagon as would be shown in the angle CDT. Here then are two figures each proven to embody the very spirit of extreme and mean proportion which, though differing in every external appearance, produce continually evidences that they are both loyal members of the great family.

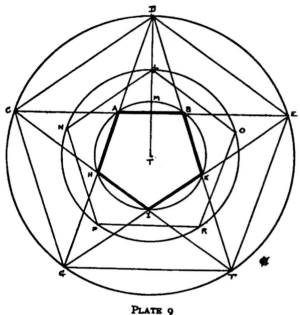

PLATE 9

PERFECTION AMPLIFIED

When we meet any one of these factors again, let us take the relationship as being understood, without argument or diagram.

History shows us many great monuments, or series of monuments which have always been the cause of endless queries as to the basis of their measurements.

In days of hoary antiquity,—long ages before Abraham the son of Terah left Ur of the Chaldees for the land of Canaan, and a thousand years ere Moses led the oppressed children from beneath the heavy hand of Pharaoh,—the inscrutable spirit of the Nile saw rising in its sacred valley in slow majesty, stone by stone, year by year, reign by reign, those imposing tombs of Gizeh, the pyramid mausoleums of Khufu, Khefren, and Menkewrē, which are among the most stable and enduring of all human structures. They symbolise many of the religious tenets of the old Egyptian faith, and typify many of their mathematical discoveries and engineering marvels. Among other things revealed to us by these proud evidences of a past glory is the advancement made by the priests in the knowledge of mathematics, one example of which is shown in their constant structural use of the figure frequently referred to in later days as the Egyptian triangle.

What may have been the origin of the proportions of this triangle we can only conjecture, since all is enveloped in the mist of dynasties crumbled and peoples long extinct. Whether it arose from an almost prehistoric knowledge of that which Euclid afterward called the "Divine Section," whether it had for these early priests a religious or only an architectural significance, and whether their knowledge was an achievement or an accident, will probably never be definitely learned; but this we do know, that the proportional members which they so persistently used in these and other monuments are wonderfully adapted to the proper adjustment of spaces in design, and have been so used from time immemorial.

There have been many archæological surveys covering the dimensions and angles of the principal pyramids, and in view of the ruinous condition of the exterior coating of most of these structures it is not unnatural to find slight diversities in their results, but we may safely take the average of several authorities as fairly illustrating the conditions. We may, however, safely state that the angle of the Egyptian Pyramid as averaged from all of the measurements comes more nearly into coincidence with the one described as being enclosed in a golden rectangle than any other. Let us therefore follow out this idea in plate 10.

If we cut the side of an Egyptian Pyramid, say Khufu, at the centre as in plate 10, and erect there, at right angles to the base, a golden rectangle with the base as its greater side (BC), and having an upright CD measured to be the corresponding lesser side, we shall have here a golden rectangle which defines the pyramid as enscribed and we shall find that the angle at the base, BCO is one of 51° 1′ and 35½″. This varies only by a minute fraction from the most exact possible measurements of a number of the pyramids, including two of the great ones at Gizeh, as shown by survey notes of repute. Is it possible that the Egyptians had no purpose in these constantly recur-

ring forms; and if they had, may we not conceive it more than probable
that they aimed at the golden proportion, the properties of which were
well known to the ancients, rather than that they had a different
object in view each time, or even that they aimed at the arbitrary

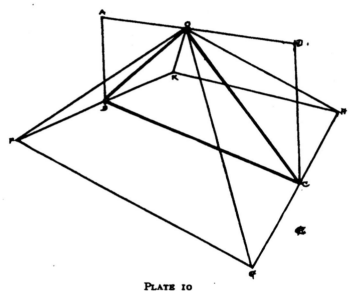

PLATE 10

PYRAMIDAL EXTREME AND MEAN PROPORTION

and less significant figures of the 5 : 8 proportion made famous centuries later by Leonardus Pisanus, and accepted by Jomard? The
figures here propounded have the merit of being highly symbolic,
well known geometrically to the ancient races, and of agreeing with
the measured conditions as nearly as the lapse of time makes possible.

When once, then, we think of the golden progressions, the Egyptian triangle and the noble pyramids of past days should arise before the mind's eye as an additional type symbolised by this great proportional group.

Before we can feel at liberty to pass away from the list of subjects illuminated by the study of this great progression, it is essential to refer more at length to the question so frequently discussed in botany under the general name of the Ideal Angle of growth.

By the ideal angle I refer to that theoretically perfect measurement at which many botanists have presumed that Nature aimed in sending out leaves, shoots, and cell formations in the early stages of development. Careful examination of the first zone of growth shows evidence that Nature's tendency in plant life is always to put forth shoots alternately at points more or less opposite the original pole, and great effort has been made by authorities on botany to arrive at a definite rule whereby the angle at which the next shoot would appear might be calculated. Many of these theories have resulted in divisions of the first zone of growth into fractional arcs of 138° or thereabouts, of which the ultimate angle at which Nature was thought to aim was called the "ideal angle."

For a great many years, numbers of botanists have endeavoured both with microscope and mathematics to determine whether these ideal angles of divergence were to be regarded in Nature's hands as a means or an end, and also to ascertain with minutest accuracy what the fractional segment of the ideal angle really was; but so far, all efforts at a definite result have been baffled by the difficulties presented in making the delicate measurements necessary to the proper application of any one of the various theories.

It is clear that, whether the relation of a series is or is not indispensable to plant growth in asymmetrical construction, Nature very surely gives constant evidence of her intention to put forth leaves and shoots at intervals which she governs; and while, as one of the authorities well says, "the numbers of the constructive curves must be integers," yet it does not follow that the fractional angle at which they are put forth must be commensurate with a *single* measurement of the circumference, as this circumference is constantly enlarging and Nature may measure as many times around the plant circle in putting forth shoots or florets as she elects before filling out the row or "coming out even" so to speak.

In order to make this explanation as brief and clear as possible, only three examples of the estimated ideal angle will be here stated. Different botanists, some comparing their theories with the Fibonacci series, have calculated the probable ideal angle at 137° 30'; 137° 30' 28"; 137° 30' 27.936". Of the three forms here set forth, the first two only are based on measurement and actual observance, the third being the equivalent of the Fibonacci series at infinity and thus theoretical only, since it represents that series at no stated step or stage but, as it might be expressed, is its composite reduced to angular form. In other words, it is what the Fibonacci series would be if it were mathematically perfect and continuing. None of the early authorities offer in support of these ideal angles much evidence other than such as can be gleaned from microscopic examination, counting of parts, and other delicate measurements too minute, too uncertain, either to prove or disprove the theories. It is natural, therefore, that all should differ in their arguments and conclusions, as well as in the mathematical rules deduced.

Arguments as to the probability or extent of Nature's use of a fixed ideal angle have been fully and learnedly carried on by botanical experts and would have no place here, but the point germane to our subject is to show, if possible, some reason which may lead to the fixing of a logical ideal angle upon a basis analogous to other known and accepted practices of Nature. Without, therefore, going into the scientific details deeply, but as being directly in point with the work in hand, I will present here in outline the substance of a theory which I suggested some years ago and which may not be without interest in this connection.

All investigations of natural phenomena proceed along one of two lines: the building of a theory upon proved facts or the construction first of a theory from analogous conditions and its subsequent support by investigation. The first method is unimpeachable where it is possible to ascertain the facts with certainty, but it is admitted by all that the accurate measurement of botanical angles is as yet unaccomplished, and this mitigates strongly against all synthetic theories and arguments concerning the ideal angle, so constructed. The second method is, however, free from this objection. That Nature continually uses extreme and mean proportion as a measuring rod is true beyond peradventure; that the resemblance between the botanically probable ideal angle (as predicated on microscopic measurements) and the limiting ratio of the Fibonacci series has been recognised; that this limiting ratio represents a hypothetical formula at infinity and not a finite condition is demonstrable; that the employment of this series in many of the investigations concerning the ideal angle has been a purely mathematical one and without the slightest recognition of Nature's continued use of an exact extreme and mean proportion in other departments is seen by examination of various works on the subject; that extreme and mean proportion is a perfect and continuing series we have already seen; and having already shown a method of determining this proportion decimally and, thereupon, angularly as well, we are in a position to declare its use by Nature wherever found, and the farther the search is carried, the more convincing is the proof that extreme and mean proportion is one of Nature's most constantly utilised measures, not only of lineal distances and as governing superficial spaces and bulk proportions but in curves and angles also. This being indisputable, the experiment of applying the angular equivalent of the extreme and mean proportion to circular growth is a natural and logical step, and the outcome is striking.

Ideal angles propounded by various authorities, as stated above:

137° 30′ : 137° 30′ 27.936″ : 137° 30′ 28″
Angular equivalent of extreme and mean proportion
137° 30′ 27.954″.—*Nature's Harmonic Unity*, p. 312.

The most casual glance will show how perfectly this angle of extreme and mean proportion, which we already know to be one of Nature's standards, coincides with the various angular forms suggested for the ideal angle, and while advancing no argument in favour of or against Nature's use of any ideal angle or series whatever, it is nevertheless not unreasonable to suppose that if and when Nature utilises any ideal angle botanically in the first or other zone of growth, whatever be the resulting form or integral count at the moment of measurement, it is highly probable that she in fact ultimately aims at the same proportional equivalent toward which she so constantly leans in her linear and superficial measurements, and I have no hesitation whatever in again claiming that when she sets out each succeeding point of growth-departure, she does so upon no permanently fixed integral basis. I venture to insist that she takes into consideration not only the position to be occupied by the identical floret chosen for examination, but the ever increasing perimeter, and that in so doing, an investigation will show every reason to accept not merely abstract figures, but the angular equivalent of extreme and mean proportion as the principle upon which she works.[1]

Accepting this is, of course, at once to understand that no accumulation of microscopic measurements could unaided establish a more fitting solution than that presented by this angular equivalent of extreme and mean proportion, perennially utilised by Nature in all branches of her creative domain.[2]

Let us illustrate what we have in mind by again referring to plate 7, wherein is shown the angular equivalent of extreme and mean proportion, and thereon base plate 11 below, from which it will be seen that the angle AOB (acute) is one of 137° 30′ 27.954″ and therefore represents not merely the golden ratio to the whole circumference as shown in plate 7 but places as well the point of growth as demonstrated by various authorities under the name of the Ideal Angle. Then, starting from B and measuring another space of the same value, we have the Ideal Angle repeated at C, this being the second point, and again repeating this process we locate the third point at D and might so continue indefinitely

[1] Appendix, Note IX.   [2] Appendix Notes to *Nature's Harmonic Unity*, page 312.

until the whole perimeter was dotted with these points of growth, each based upon an absolutely perfect extreme and mean proportion and each being the logical point as shown above. For diagrammatic purposes it is perhaps interesting to note that the point D (third stage of the circular progress) marks, well within the limit of accurate

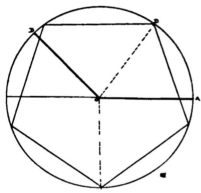

PLATE 11

THE IDEAL ANGLE AND THE GOLDEN SERIES

drawing, the position of the corner of the inscribed pentagon, if drawn with its apex downward. (Appendix, Note V[c]).

Before going on to specific examples where we shall find the members of the two families, the Tetragon Family and the Pentagon Family, in constant evidence, let us summarise some of the proofs which we have accumulated and which we may therefore hereafter safely omit throughout this work.

In the Tetragon Family, we have satisfied ourselves that whenever we find evidences of the square, the octagon, the equilateral triangle, the hexagon, or their progressions or rectangles, we may safely infer that other coincidences of the same kind would follow were we to diagram them, but that simplicity and clarity will be furthered by the omission of all but one element in each diagram, considering the rest to follow as a matter of course.

In the Pentagon Family, we have likewise, I trust, satisfied ourselves that, between the numerical, the linear, the superficial, and the solid measurements of the golden ratio on the one hand, and the pentagon, the pentagram, the Egyptian Pyramid, and the Ideal Angle on the other, a relationship exists so striking and continuous that, once granting the fact that extreme and mean proportion is the governing element of a structure, further evidence need not be introduced to obscure the main feature, these allied factors being, like our innocence of crime, taken for granted until the contrary be proved.

By the use of this *prima facie* case, the statement of future matters will be simplified almost beyond belief and may safely be indulged in since, where it is desirable to express limitations, there will be no difficulty in doing so.

SPIRAL FORMATION

The circle has, time out of mind, been considered the symbol of Divinity. In its proportion, its balance, its ever turning about upon itself, it is the human ideal and the mathematical type of a fully formed self-sufficiency in which further progress is unnecessary if not impossible. Hence, we so frequently find Nature preferring that other curvilinear form known as the spiral, the property of which is a continued, never-satisfied progress, being thus the mathematical type of a growth which may extend indefinitely until cut off by forces beyond its own limitations. John Ruskin has said that the line of beauty is an infinite line, not returning on itself. Of nothing could this be more true than of the spirals.

Nature's use of spirals, and their inherent beauty are, perhaps, matters of daily observance, yet it does not follow necessarily that, however important and familiar they may be, spirals of themselves form a family. Spirals may,—must in fact,—all be measured in the final analysis by angles, and the angular families into which we have found natural phenomena grouping themselves will serve to subdivide spirals into their various branches just as accurately as they do the other geometric figures to which they have been applied. Indeed, a vast majority of the spirals of Nature will be found to fall at once and indisputably into the great growth-family of extreme and mean proportion, as may be gleaned from a study of the examples shown in *Nature's Harmonic Unity*[1]; and for all of these reasons, spirals together with catenary curves, may safely and conveniently be treated

[1] See Chapter on Spirals and Asymmetry later in this work.

as part of the composite whole, separated for convenience perhaps but not for any reason which excludes them from the same distinguishing differences that obtain in other forms.

SUMMARY

In spite of the fact that our examination of the geometric figures symbolising the various families has so far proceeded on perfect numerical sequence from the line to the trigon, thence to the tetragon and the pentagon, let us not rashly jump to the conclusion that the process should or can be infinitely prolonged. The basic principle may be said in a very definite way to terminate with the pentagon, not merely from the necessity of terminating it somewhere and selecting the pentamerous form as being the first plausible period, but for other and far more substantial reasons, only a few of which it seems worth while to outline; and if we have, from time to time regarded the hexagon and octagon, it will be seen that these have only been included as sublimated products of the equilateral triangle and the square.

It has already been remarked as of primal importance that no general principle which treated Nature as composed of plane surfaces only would be either sufficient or safe, and, since this is so, we must, in all of our applications, take solid formations into consideration: and while it is obviously true that solids may take any form, yet in the very nature of our study, regular solids present the simplest basis of examination, nor shall we, in such a work as this, be able to pursue the geometric foundation much beyond that point. The ancients well knew the limit of the regular polyhedral angles, and Albrecht Dürer, student, artist, mathematician, and the patron of exactness, recognised this thoroughly in his work on geometry[1]; and in order to get a fair idea of the situation, let us state a few of the accepted facts, and clothe them in the simplest possible garments.

It is clear that if two angles of ninety degrees be placed back to back as in figure A, plate 12, their bases will form one and the same straight line, and it follows that any combination of angles, the sum of which equals one hundred and eighty degrees (the sum of two right angles) will, as shown in figure B of the same plate, form a continuous base. Further, it is simple and indisputable that if the sum of the angles so formed is in excess of one hundred and eighty degrees, as is the case illustrated in figure C, plate 12, then the line heretofore continuous will be bent back into an indentation, having become what, in military construction we call a re-entrant angle. Pursuing the same process farther, we see that if four angles be grouped about a common point as shown in figure E, of the same plate, they cannot exceed in their aggregate the sum of three hundred and sixty degrees (the sum of four right angles) and still lie flat in a plane. If these angles aggregate less than this sum, they will necessarily rise to a

[1] Libella Quatuor Institutionum Geometricarum. *See also* Appendix, Note IX.

5

point at their apex and form a pyramid, and carrying the logic a step beyond this we see that if the aggregate exceeds the sum mentioned, then the result can only be conceived as producing a depression or indentation in the plane similar in effect to the indentation in the line shown in figure C of this plate.

The conclusion then, is inevitable, that no regular solid can be formed of angles which, coming to a common point or apex, equal or exceed an aggregate of three hundred and sixty degrees, since to equal this sum would produce a flat surface or plane and to exceed it would produce by complement a depression and not an apex.

Applying this principle to the geometrical figures which have so far been the basis of our studies, we shall find that in the case of the equilateral triangle, we may make combinations showing three triangles at an apex, with a total of three times sixty or one hundred and eighty degrees, four triangles with a total of two hundred and forty degrees, or five triangles, with a total of three hundred degrees. All of these are possible, as illustrated in the figures of the tetrahedron (figure G, plate 12) the octahedron (figure K) and the icosahedron (figure L), but there we are forced to stop so far as the equilateral triangle is concerned, since six angles of sixty degrees aggregate three hundred and sixty degrees, and, as shown in figure D of this plate, form a flat surface and no apex or summit whatever.[1]

[1] *See* Appendix, Note X.

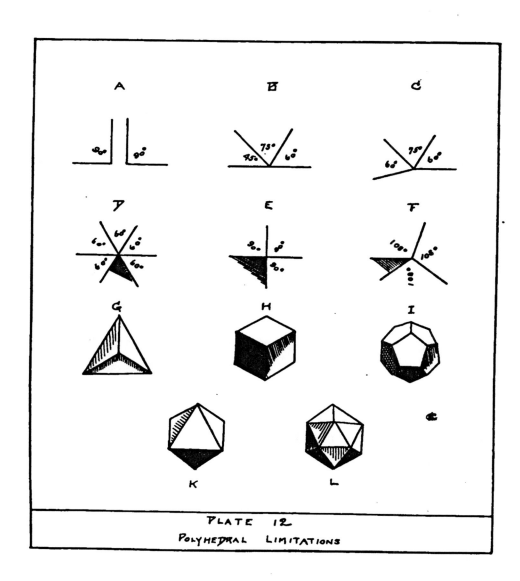

PLATE 12

POLYHEDRAL LIMITATIONS

In a square or rectangle having corners of ninety degrees, three may be combined to form a solid as in figure H, showing a cube or hexahedron, but with four of these we arrive at the same result produced by six equiangular triangles,—a flat plane. The pentagon is, we know, formed of angles of one hundred and eight degrees at each corner. Placing three of these around a common point, as in figure F, we see that the sum of the three, being three hundred and twenty-four degrees, still leaves a balance in favour of a vertex, which permits the formation of a regular polyhedral solid known as the dodecahedron, illustrated in figure I of the plate mentioned, but no further step can be taken with the pentagon as an additional angle exceeds the limit described.

Coming now to the hexagon of one hundred and twenty degrees, we see at a glance that, while two planes formed of these will be insufficient to enclose space, three will in turn produce a mere flat plane as did six equilateral triangles, and no vertex will be formed. The same is, *a fortiore*, true of the heptagon, and of all figures having a greater number of angles. When therefore the hexagon is found in the formation of crystals and other natural forms, it is invariably either as a decorator of flat surfaces, or in conjunction with geometrical configurations other than itself, such as its relatives in the tetragon family.

We may briefly conclude, therefore, that, while irregular solids may be formed in any number of combinations, yet, as these are of great complexity, and as art and architecture seldom have recourse to them in the proportioning of their spaces, we should not be justified in going beyond the lines laid down in the above investigation since, in these pages, even the hexagon and the octagon are touched upon largely in connection with the measurement of forces or linear distances, or in relation to the decoration of such flat surfaces as snow crystals,[1] and then, indeed, only as being cousins-German to the equilateral triangle and the square, and as necessary and beautiful sojourners within the camp of the Tetragon Family, *but not as forming a family by themselves.*

Carrying, then, this plan to its logical conclusion, we shall find that in the end we may simplify our comparisons by dividing all processes roughly into two great classes as originally shown, the numerical and the geometric. As we have seen, the former may be subdivided, the first sub-group comprising those arithmetical progressions to which attention has been called, but which, in fact, occur much more frequently in mathematics than in Nature; and the second group being typified by the Fibonacci series by which we find Nature constantly ticking off her numbered and completed factors in the progress of increase. The geometric class or process yields, as emphasised, most prominently the three family groups in its subdivision,

[1] See further details of hexagonal formations in the Appendix, Note XI.

the Tetragon or square and the golden series, symbolised by the pentagon and the asymmetric group; and falling into one or other of these three we shall find a large majority of the forms and phenomena of Nature which will come under our notice. Amongst the Tetragon group will be placed the infinite variety of examples furnished by gravity, force, and dynamics,[1] while under vital influences we shall find the magic of the extreme and mean ratio constantly exhibited. Other forms will call for a passing notice; other configurations will, perhaps, be separately examined for the sake of convenience, as will be the case with ellipses and a number of other curves but in the end nearly all of these will be found to have taken their allotted places as admeasured by one or other of the groups to which our attention has been devoted. It might, indeed, almost be said that without these was nothing made that was made. They are THE GREAT MODULES.

[1] Appendix, Note XXXIII.

CHAPTER III

THE TRIGON IN VISIBLE NATURE

A S gravity and polar force are such vast and universal powers and constantly exercising their influence over whatever possesses physical attributes, there would be perhaps some academic advantage in placing next in order a chapter setting forth the evidence to prove that these forces are governed by rules coming under the tetragon and trigon group. Efforts however to catch the attention relative to mere invisible force are of extreme difficulty, and in order first to introduce to the reader some of the visible beauties upon which this series of rules is brought to bear the tangible has been given precedence over the intangible in the hope that thus, fixing interest first on the visible demonstrations, the unseen and more abstruse matters of force may safely be left for a succeeding chapter after the general working of the plan is more clearly illustrated.

Recognising then that as all members of this tetragon group have been found to support certain features in common, and that as shown in the preceding chapter, once it be satisfactorily demonstrated that an object is proportioned on the square, we can instantly feel assured that the equilateral triangle and the hexagon will, at their appointed places assume their wonted responsibilities, it will be interesting to see how these things work out in practice and whether these points develop in fact as well as they do in theory.

Perhaps in all created things no more beautiful example of the workings of the laws of polar force, or more perfect hexagonal design could be found than in one of the whirling snow flakes formed and re-formed while making its one terrestrial journey from the dull, grey, wintry cloud that conceived it, through a few short seconds to the drift where it joins its storm-born mates. Bear in mind that, though a lifetime were spent in the search, no two of these spectacular beauties would ever be found exactly alike, none of them last more than a few seconds, none of them have been more than a fraction of a minute in their formation; they are engraved and etched and beaded and carved beyond the power of the microscope to investigate them; they have been falling from the heavens since man came on earth and will continue to fall so long as temperatures vary. Yet never one in all of these milliards of millions that varied from the form of a hexagon or showed a pattern which was not a six-cornered exemplar of the Tetragon Family.

Suppose we look carefully at a number of examples of snow crystals taken from the wonderful collection of photographs made by W. A. Bently of Vermont. It is hardly necessary to indulge in very

PLATE 13

SNOW CRYSTAL

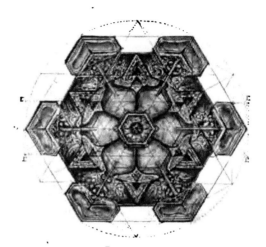

PLATE 14

SNOW CRYSTAL

PLATE 15

SNOW CRYSTAL

PLATE 16

SNOW CRYSTAL

The above illustrations are taken from *Nature's Harmonic Unity*.

PLATE 17

SNOW CRYSTAL

extended comment as the illustrations themselves proclaim their origin and family in every line.

It can hardly be without great additional interest to note that plate 16 is an extremely magnified photograph of the interior concentric portion of the decoration on the same snow crystal shown more completely, though on smaller scale, in plate 17 nor has any photographic apparatus yet been devised which discloses the slightest waning in the exactness and beauty of these concentric diagrams.

While the rock crystals and crystals of various salts and chemical combinations furnish an endless array of interesting subjects, they are nevertheless difficult of examination from a mere drawing, being many-sided solids which at best present but a confused mass of lines to the eye in an illustration. It is possible, however, in some of the simpler forms to show clearly how crystals, whatever be their nature, conform to the great rules laid down by polar force and gravity and this can scarcely be better illustrated than by showing the two plates 18 and 19 wherein are given end views of crystals of cuprus uranite and dolomite.

As we progress upwards in the scale to animate life we rise first from the inanimate crystals to the lower orders, wherein must be classed the *algeæ*. Among the monocellulars are many forms of vegetable life formerly considered to be minute animals, developing with a marvellous rapidity, an incredible number finding ample space in a teaspoonful of water. They have been given the name of diatoms (Diatomaceæ) from their habit of propagation by a simple division, thus creating two atoms where only one was before. These beautiful

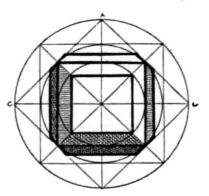 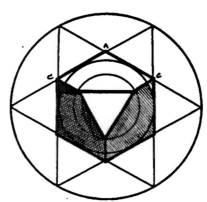

PLATE 18—CUPRUS URANITE   PLATE 19—DOLOMITE

Bacillariaceæ are engraved and etched with the same care as the snow crystals, and instances are not lacking where the lines of engraving in the decoration have been microscopically traced and counted to the number of 125,000 to the inch. We may say that our knowledge of these decorations is limited as in other cases only by the possibility of the instrument to make them visible by magnification. These beautiful things take the forms of all of the polyhedra but in the majority of cases the patterns are limited to triangular and hexagonal ones as shown in the illustrations in plates 20, 21, 22, and 23. Occasionally one is seen which shows the direct tendencies of the square

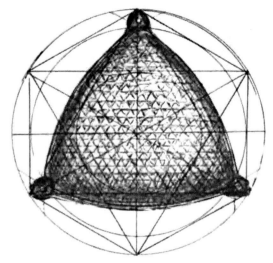

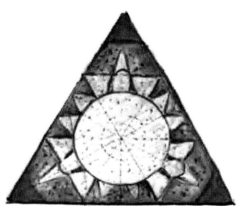

PLATE 20
TRIANGULAR DIATOM

PLATE 21
TRIANGULAR DIATOM

PLATE 22
HEXAGONAL DIATOM

PLATE 23
HEXAGONAL DIATOM

Diatom Illustrations as taken from *Nature's Harmonic Unity.*

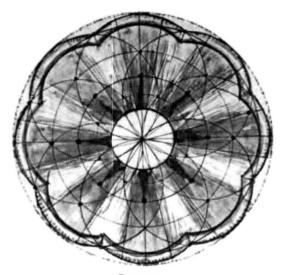

PLATE 24
OCTAGONAL DIATOM

PLATE 25
OCTAGONAL DIATOM

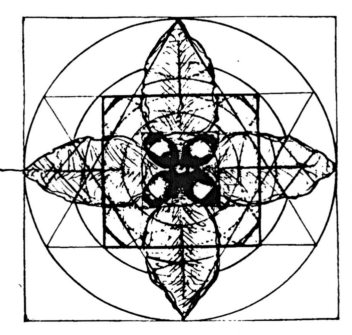

PLATE 26
SEPALS AND SEED VESSELS OF SYRINGA

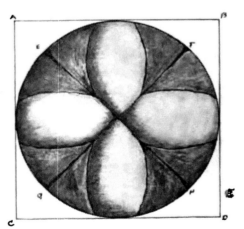

PLATE 28
COTTON

and the octagon, as in plates 24 and 25, all of which will explain themselves immediately upon a comparison with the plates contained in Chapter I.

Rising now from these lower orders to the higher forms of plant life, we find the same tendency strong within flowers familiar to us all. Of these, attention is first invited to two in which the direct factor is evidently the tetragon or square. In plate 26 we see a drawing of the sepals and seed vessels of the syringa in which the four sepals are carried out by four seed vessels and these in proportion are governed by the fourth progression of the prime square. Again we turn to plate 27 showing Onagra Biennis, with its four leaves and a central circle coinciding with the fourth progression of the square, and again in the bursting cotton, as shown in plate 28, is seen a most definite instance of the same relationship to rectangular form.

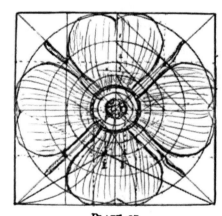

PLATE 27

ONAGRA BIENNIS

No examination of plant life under the influence of the laws of polar force and the tetragonal family would however be complete without some of the beautiful illustrations which constantly occur in the six-sided flowers such as the jonquil (plate 29) and the tiger lily (plate 30), to which might well be added Zygadenus Elegans and the Easter lily (plates 83 and 84), *Nature's Harmonic Unity*, in each of which the flower petals lie in the form of the equilateral triangle like a babe in its crib, while the inner markings are defined by the regular progressions of the hexagon as indicated in the plates.

There is, however, a stage in natural development which is high above that of plant and vegetation and this is the life of animate things, and these we must examine briefly. Look for a moment at the beautiful butterfly illustrated in plate 31 and then consider again the wonderful exactness of the equilateral triangle formed by his powdered wings.

And if these were not enough, inspect please, the work of the wasp in forming his remarkable nest (plate 32) and the marvellous comb of the common honey bee (plate 33) with its perfect building and ultimate utility and hexagonal economy.

In creating her remarkable wax storehouse, Mr. Bigelow, in his recent issue of *The Guide to Nature*, disowns the theory long upheld, that the bee really goes about this cell building with any plan to create a series of hexagonal cells. He says that "in making the comb the honey-bees never work in hexagons but always in circles. Then she keeps going into the cell like a gun swab and pushes out the sides, and it is this pressure on the sides, with not the slightest intent nor

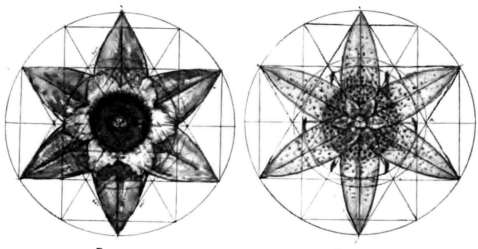

PLATE 29
JONQUIL

PLATE 30
TIGER LILY

PLATE 31
BUTTERFLY AND THE TRIGON

skill on the bee's part, but purely the effect of a mathematical law, that makes the hexagon." In these conclusions, as will be shown in the appendix, Mr. Bigelow has some supporters and many opponents; and for myself, while I am quite prepared to admit that from an

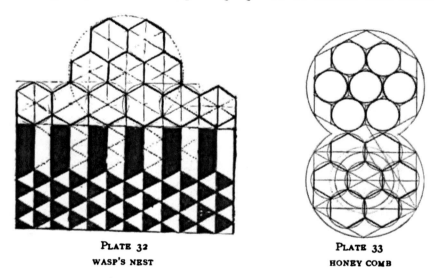

PLATE 32
WASP'S NEST

PLATE 33
HONEY COMB

architectural standpoint, it is highly likely that Mrs. Bee never thinks of her storehouse as a hexagon—or as a circle either for the matter of that; that she has neither ground plan nor elevation, blue print nor trowel, and that her "intentions" can only be guessed from the results produced; but if she can build circular cells and then change them into architecturally economic hexagons in the process of plunging back and forth to fill them, she is even a better economist than we had given her credit for.   The result is one of the marvels of creation, and whether the bee or Mother Nature shall have the most of the credit is small matter.   You can scarcely fail to read with interest, in view of this development, the account of the investigation made by the great Réaumur many years ago on the same subject.

"They have solved," says Réaumur, "a very difficult problem of geometry, for only a limited material or wax is at their disposal for the construction of their house, the rooms or cells of which must be of a determined capacity of the largest size, and with the strongest walls in proportion to the amount of matter to be employed. . . . The cylindrical form would seem to be the best adapted to the shape of the bee's body, but this would leave vacant or waste room between the contiguous cells; on the other hand, had the cells been square or triangular, they might have been constructed without so many unnecessary vacancies, still they would have required more material and then would not have fitted the body of the insect. . . . The six-sided form of the hexagon fulfils the problem in every particular; the base of each cell, instead of forming a plane, is composed of three diamond shaped pieces placed in such a manner as to produce a shallow pyramid, which structure imparts greater strength while giving a larger capacity with the smallest expenditure of time and material. The angles of these cells on the longest space measure 109° 28′ and on the smallest 70° and 32'." The angle as measured by Réaumur as nearly as might be in the bee's actual work varies only infinitesimally from the one which we are told produces the greatest strength for the least expenditure of materials in building, or perhaps, indeed, differs not at all. The above story of Réaumur has also been told in many versions, connecting it with the scientist König and others. Réaumur, it is said, desiring to learn how exactly the work of the bee conformed to the requirements of abstract science, consulted the figures of Maraldi as to what the angles should be to give the greatest capacity for the least amount of comb and found, in answer, the figures 109° 26' for the greater and 70° 34' for the lesser. Puzzled by the slight difference between the actualities which had been observed and the theoretical perfection which the mathematical answer required, it is said that the academic question was later put to König, upon whose reply, naturalists finally determined that the original figures and neither those of science nor the bee were at fault.[1] Whatever account of this episode be accepted, the fact remains that, somehow, the bee produces cell walls which comply in structural form with the last dictates of science, and it is wonderfully instructive to see how frequently it comes about that a bold statement to the effect that Nature is working at cross purposes or is less inspired than we thought

[1] For further details of this Nature-wonder and other hexagonal cell formations, *see* Appendix, Note XII.

her to have been, proves on investigation merely to be the means of disclosing carelessness in assembling evidence on the part of the critic himself.

The examination of the Tetragon Family in Nature cannot, perhaps, be brought to a focus more suitably than by the presenting of the four following illustrations, in the first of which (plate 34) we have an example of the orien-

PLATE 34
JAPANESE IRIS
The Triangle (Korin)

PLATE 35
DANISH-CROSS POPPY
The Square

PLATE 36
ANEMONE CORONARIA
Hexagon

PLATE 37
SINGLE DAHLIA
Octagon

tal iris after the drawings of the famous Japanese artist Ogata Korin, who saw this beautiful flower in all its obvious triangularity as long ago as 1675, when he led the art of Nippon and, disregarding the existing conventions, made for himself a name which has not yet faded, drawing those beautiful screen designs with which we are so familiar and which embody so many of these delightful blossoms. True to mythology, Iris bears a message from his day to our own.

In plate 35, a four-petalled Danish-Cross poppy, scarlet of bowl and silver-white of centre, presses its tetragonal significance not merely through the number of its petals but through its symbolic cross as well. Following this, in plate 36, are shown examples of the six-membered anemone coronaria, brilliant as red blood and renowned through the ages as being those lilies of the field of which we read that they toil not neither do they spin, yet that Solomon in all his glory was not arrayed like one of these.

Finally, in plate 37, we have the astonishingly regular and almost self-conventionalised blossoms of the single dahlia. Trained to assume many colours and many forms in many climes, yet in all its vicissitudes and wanderings and changes, we recognise one persistent characteristic in its determination always to be eight petalled when left to its own devices. Thus the dahlia, with its companions, round out the theme of floral symbols in which we see portrayed the equilateral triangle, the square, the hexagon, and the octagon, botanically typifying the chapter in its entirety, and fittingly concluding this portion of our subject.

CHAPTER IV [1]

THE TRIGON IN FORCE

THE examination of the beautiful and innumerable flowers, crystals, diatoms, and other forms illustrative of natural development along the lines of the trigon and the tetragon, a few representatives of which we have seen in the foregoing chapter, must not, charming as they are, blind us to the fact that Nature has in reserve for us if we will but look for them, still more stupendous and awe-inspiring things in store.

So far, our examination of the principles enunciated has been confined to the materialistic side of the question and has necessarily restricted itself to outward and visible forms in which the signs were outward and visible also, and in which demonstration and proof of the simplest ocular kind was all that was necessary. Let us now recognise, however, that all of the tangible and visible beauty within our ken, all the beauty in the world indeed, is fundamentally rooted and founded in a few basic factors or properties or forces which are, themselves, invisible.

[1] Chapter taken from *The Great Modules*, C. Arthur Coan, 1914.

Choose we the opera, where we drink in artificial beauty through the senses, or choose we the forest, where the birds of the air hold us rapt with the beauty of their feather and song, or go we where we will, beauty takes ever its most potent charm from one of four factors,— form, motion, colour, or sound. A moment's thought shows us that, like most material things, these concurrent factors arise, one and all, from a government of the invisible. As invisible and intangible vibration control both the colour and sound which please us, so gravity in large measure governs both the form and motion of the component items of the picture. Sound and light, which beget music and colour, belong alike to the transitory, illusive, and non-substantial world wherein gravitation and heat and other forms of force play, like mischievous elves, with things substantial. These forces possess none of the properties of matter, are not subject to contraction, expansion, or cohesion; they have neither length, breadth, nor thickness; are made up of neither molecules nor atoms, nor have they other material attributes, yet are recognisable by man through the nicely adjusted senses with which he has been endowed by his Creator, since they set in motion, by their invisible power, these things visible.

GRAVITY

We are very prone to define gravity as an intangible force which attracts all things to the earth, forgetting that we deal with one of those rules which work both ways with equal regularity. In proportion to the mass of the object, the misty cloud draws the earth upwards with the same steadfast purpose that the more solid earth draws the vapour down to itself. The apparent difference grows altogether out of the variance in amount of matter exerting the influence. Let us clearly understand this, then, that gravity signifies the remarkable power exerted by every particle of matter upon every other particle. A few million years ago Dame Nature penned the rules which were to govern her realm. This code she wrote in indelible ink on the first page of her original report and there it remains, a model statute to this day, like unto the law of the Medes and Persians which altereth not; and among other interesting things she said that every smallest atom of matter should ever and always exercise this strange and benign influence over every other atom, however distant, and that all substance should forever have a tendency to come together. Without it, worlds and their contents and inhabitants would fly apart, and Waller expresses it very concisely when he writes of

"The chain that's fixed to the throne of Jove,
    On which the fabrick of the world depends;
    One link dissolved, the whole creation ends."

This gravity then is an invisible force which is exerted upon every atom of matter in the universe, whether that atom be itself visible or invisible; and this gravity, which may be considered as being in a sense a "polar force," we must comprehend as working in two ways and under opposite influences at one and the same time. It is not magnetism, though by many confused with it, yet under the spell of this universal magician, bends every twig of the forest and by its command rolls every billow of the sea. By grace of its steadfast laws, every planet in the heavens pursues its stately course and every midge that flies darts airily through the silver moonlight: the curves of the mountain are its sign and the angles of the crystal are its signet: unsubstantial itself, it governs all substance, and unseen, it is monarch of all things visible.

We may then view all things in Nature as having been influenced in their formation by this great force. In the inorganic forms, where exterior influences are less marked and where the interpolation of other laws of growth and formation are less intruding, we shall find, as seen in the previous chapter, a constant tendency to assume, under the influence of this polar force, permanent forms of the tetragon family of which we have spoken. Nor must we allow ourselves to suppose that this tendency terminates with the visibility which enables us to see so readily that the snow crystal is a hexagon. We must, on the contrary, remember that this continues indefinitely through all of the tests to which we can put invisible force.

If our theory be true, then it must be possible to demonstrate not merely that gravity act as unequivocally in the stellar spaces as it does on the earth, but also that in matters astronomical we shall find frequent evidence of the trigonal tendency. Let us try this out by examining the solar system for a few minutes and see what we shall see. For this purpose, we shall select our own planetary system, both because it is nearest at hand and includes our little world, and also because its motions are so much more obvious and its distances so much more accurately measurable than those of the stars which we, with our finite and childlike simplicity call, "fixed."

If we start our examination with plate 38 in which the positions of the planets more distant from the sun than our own are depicted, we must first accept the fact that for purposes of popular demonstration the orbits have been platted in their circular equivalents, rather than in the slightly elliptical form in which we know that they actually occur. This is a liberty taken in many a reputable map of astronomy and serves to clarify the illustrative purpose without in any wise prejudicing the accuracy, since, for accuracy we are not dependent on the illustration but have recourse to the logarithmic proofs deduced from accepted tables. Examining the plate, then, of the planets of which the most outwardly one is Neptune, and approaching the sun through the paths of those whose mean vectors exceed that of the earth, and which planets, for that reason are called "superior," we find that three progressions of the hexagon bring us on the illustration, from the position of Neptune to that of Uranus; five more, from Uranus to Saturn; four more from Saturn to Jupiter, and so on.   You will perhaps say in regard to these illustrations, that they could easily be made up to suit the occasion, and really prove nothing, since a demonstration on paper the size of this page would be utterly lacking in accuracy. To this I respond that, were I to have presented to you such a proof, you would indeed be justified in throwing the book out of the most convenient window. I depend, on the contrary, upon nothing so superficial, nothing so futile. The plates are inserted merely to illuminate the demonstration resulting from a scientific comparison of the theory with the facts. We know the mean or average distances of the planets from the sun as generally accepted by reputable astronomers. It is also mathematically and astronomically simple to visualise the heavens as mapped out into the hexagonal progressions which are now under our consideration. The true geometric distances between these outlines can be calculated by their radii with an accuracy even greater than that with which it is possible to determine the positions of the stars themselves; and in this web we can place the planets in their orbits with a nicety limited only by the ability of the astronomer to tell us what the exact distances of the planets from the sun really are.

If I am right that Nature, in apportioning the celestial spaces, shows a strong tendency to accept the members of the tetragon

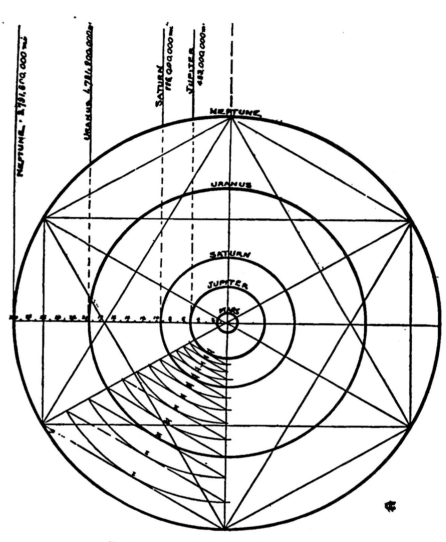

PLATE 38—ORBITS OF THE SUPERIOR PLANETS

THE NUMBERS ON THE HORIZONTAL DIAMETER ARE ASTRONOMICAL UNITS OR MULTIPLES OF THE
DISTANCE OF THE EARTH FROM THE SUN AND ARE NOT MEASUREMENTS OF MILES.

89

family which so largely govern gravity, as her foot rule, then the figures deduced from a comparison of these two methods should reasonably coincide. If now, the known distances as tabulated should be found really coincident with the calculated distances as determined from the heavens so mapped, then it is fair to infer that reason supports the claim and any theory so supported is not unworthy consideration.

Let us conceive our plate as representing the heavens so mapped by this imaginary web stretching with absolute accuracy across them, and stretching with sufficient accuracy across our tiny page, and then let us make a brief trigonometrical examination of the facts. The authorities tell us that the mean distance of Neptune from the sun (for his distance is not always the same by a good shot) is two billion, seven hundred ninety-six million miles; Uranus, one billion, seven hundred eighty-four million, with Saturn about half that and Jupiter about half the distance of Saturn, while Mars is only once and a half the distance from the sun that Earth maintains, and so, by comparison with most of the others may be considered a near neighbour. Taking this as a basis for our diagram, we have placed Neptune at the required position on the outermost or prime circle, basing its radius on the known position of the planet. Spare me then the moments necessary to examine the others in their positions with relation to the great orb of day; Uranus on the circle of the third progression of the hexagon, created as described in our opening chapter; Saturn next, on the fifth beyond; Jupiter still four progressions nearer the sun; and Mars, innermost, being in fact too near the centre for convenient consideration on so small a plate, so that we shall take up the Martian question later with greater magnification. Our plate 38 shows us all of these things as being *fait accompli*, just as I have described them. Now let us apply to these positions as indicated by the hexagonal progressions, the hard and unsympathetic test of unyielding mathematics and learn where our planets, so placed in imagination, would in fact be found in the stellar system. I will tell you briefly. Astronomers themselves differ, and in some instances, differ by a serious number of millions of miles, as to stellar distances. I have before me, for example, two highly reputable calculations of the position of Neptune, differing from each other by well over eight million miles. When we talk then, of accuracy, it must be with the understanding that even the doctors do not always agree: so, in some instances every theory varies at times from any given authority, and ours is no exception to the rule, but it differs less than many of these authorities vary from each other. Again, let me say, that the greatest and least distances of any given planet from the sun in the course of its regular orbital revolution, differ much more from each other than the same planet's distance as calculated from our hexagonal diagram would differ from the measured average distance or radius of the same star: and finally, let me add, that more than one recognised, accepted, and useful theory in astronomy when put to a test, is found, like Bode's Law, to vary from the details much more widely than does the theory before us. The calculations upon which one must rely to support such statements as these, however meritorious, are deadly dull, and they have been sent to the accessible if unobtrusive limbo of the appendix.[1]

In order to make the matter still clearer, let us add a short examination of plate 39 in which we continue the process above described by diagramming the comparative distances separating the so-called "inferior" planets from each other and from the sun itself, and our drawing is practically a magnified edition of the interior circle of the previous plate with the orbit of Mars now enlarged so that we may study the planets nearer the sun. Here we learn that, measured by their own mean vectors, the distance of Mars, with his red and glaring eye, from our Earth, which shines to all of the others with a colour at which we can only guess, is laid off accurately by three progressions of the hexagon, while, as detailed in the mathematical notes, charming Venus, the changeable lady who meant Hesperus and Phorphorus by turns to the ancients, lies on the other side of us and nearer the sun by four and Mercury, the sandalled bearer of the caduceus, by eight tetragonal units, looking straight into the eye of the great sun.

[1] Appendix, Note XIII.

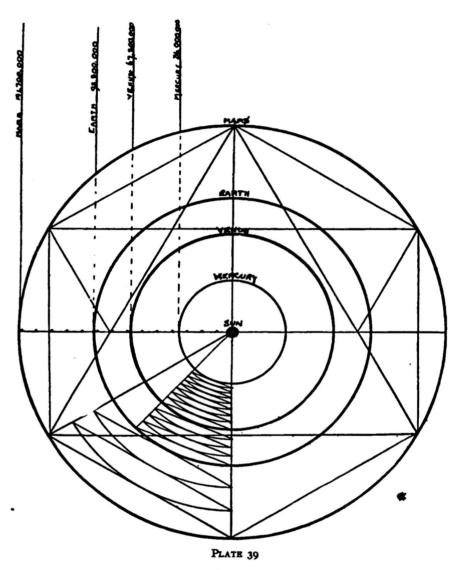

PLATE 39

ORBITS OF THE INFERIOR PLANETS WITH MARS

93

Were one disposed to scoff at speculations such as these, it needs only to go back to the study of this same law of Bode, to which we referred, and the discovery of the asteroids by its observation, to find ample reason restraining caustic comment. There are several points with regard to this theory of Bode, which are of interest to us. In the first place, it happens that it was not Bode's Law at all, having been publicly announced by a more retiring and modest astronomer, one Johann Daniel Titius of Wittenberg, several years before it was boldly appropriated by the Berlin professor, Bode, and given his name. Next, as has been hinted above, it is, when put to the acid test, only generically and not specifically, correct, being, in one case at least, that of Neptune, notably incorrect. In spite of these handicaps, however, and impugned, as it were, both as to its honesty and its veracity, yet, so great is the underlying truth of the theory, that wonders were worked in its name, and who can say what other wonders its future will aid in disclosing, even to the existence of a ninth planet seventy-seven times as far from the sun as our familiar Earth.

Titius of Wittenberg, you will perhaps remember, announced that he had discovered certain relations between the distances of the various planets from the sun, but neither he nor Bode carried these beyond the point of building upon them a numerical series in which the distance of Earth from the sun was used as a measuring rod, as is not unusual, and called an astronomical unit. Setting down a series of fours and adding multiples of threes with the powers of two, and decimally dividing by ten, we shall have, as totals, the distances of the various planets from the sun as expressed in these astronomical units, thus summarising Bode's Law.

☿	♀	⊕	♂		♃	♄	♄	♅	?
4,	4,	4,	4,	4,	4,	4,	4,	4,	4,
0	3	6	12	24	48	96	192	384	768
.4	.7	1.0	1.6	2.8	5.2	10.0	19.6	38.8	77.2

Can it now be stated that such a table shows accurately the positions of the planets? With absolute accuracy? No. Nevertheless, the figures do bear a remarkable similarity to the facts. Now observe that this law was first announced to the world in 1772 and that at that time the interval between the position of Mars at approximately one and six-tenths astronomical units from the sun and Jupiter at five and two-tenths, was still unexplained, and ne'ther Uranus nor Neptune had been discovered. Then, visualise Herschel as discovering Uranus, which for a while bore his name. The edge was somewhat taken off this discovery by the fact that, for a considerable time it was supposed that the new heavenly traveller was a comet and not until later was it determined that a planet had been added to our system. When, however, it was known that Uranus was a planet, interest instantly centred around the question of its position in relation to

Bode's Law and we now know that it fell as exactly into its appointed spot as if the placing of chairs at the celestial table for unexpected wanderers were a matter of daily occurrence. Since a planet was obligingly found to fill every niche in the system except that between Mars and Jupiter, what more natural then, than that speculation should be rife as to why nothing appeared to occupy this one existing cavity and make the system perfect. Universal search along these lines was quickly rewarded, and today we have, as a result, the records of hundreds of asteroids, little broken particles of a once-planet which circled around the sun in the orbit now vacant but for them. That, however, was not all, for the same research led to the final placing of Neptune, the outermost and farthest distant of all of the known planets, making his majestic tour around the sun once in one hundred and sixty-four years, and circling in that cold darkness thirty-odd times as far from the sun as the little Earth we tread. [1]

Thus we emphasise the value of careful, scientific speculation, and at the same time we add to the facts as covered by the law of Bode the further item, that the progressive distances between the planets are not only governed, as shown by Titius, by a law, of which he gave us a numerical theory, but that that law when analysed shows these distances to be conformable with an astonishing fidelity to the progressions of the tetragon family as we have diagrammed them;

[1] Appendix, Note XIV.

and that this is only one more of the many instances in which the effects of gravity are found to fall into this classification.

Before leaving the study of the force of gravity and going on separately to other forces, let us for a moment see how this attractive power which holds the world together compares in its operation with other invisible agents such as sound and light. It is, I need not repeat, one of the purposes of this work to show that Nature is one grandly consistent whole rather than a series of harmonic accidents. She is no group of separate entities, working either severally or in partnership; she is no merely articulated collection of units, with a set of laws governing chemistry, and another set controlling sound, a separate set governing biology and opposite rules dominating light. Additional codes she has which, being compounds of other laws, govern compounds of correlated facts, but my contention has always been that the great thread of her power runs through the whole fabric consistently and harmoniously, and that each science and each art is therefore a mere branch of the whole, inseparable in its final perfection from the remainder. Her laws of gravity apply, as we have seen, throughout all the universe, confining themselves neither to one science nor even to one world. In the same way all the laws of sound, light, and radiant energy apply wherever vibrations may occur, whether on this little planet or another, or in the incalculable inter-stellar spaces between them.

7

Having noticed this universality of the operation of natural laws, it is but a step to comprehend that we may expect to find that even the laws themselves and the forces which they govern, have a unity of purpose and a similarity in structure, and that gravity and sound and light, for example, have more in common than at first we credit them. To prove this is equivalent to stating that there are universal laws which have much to do with beauty, since we have already observed that all beauty arises in a sense-appeal; and this is possible only through those reactions which, as has been stated, depend on form and motion, the latter including all vibratory sensations such as colour and sound. To the Horatios who pursue life at a dead-level, never venturing into the uncertain realms of speculation, Hamlet stands as a prophet. There are, indeed, more things in heaven and earth than are dreamt of in their philosophy.

In olden times, times perhaps as long past as Egypt, the intellectuals, who were also the high priests, the surgeons, the painters, and the writers of that noble land,—searched diligently for means of producing the brilliant and haunting colours needed for their work; and prominent among these researches came their effort to produce the effect of heraldic gold or purple without extravagant use of the virgin metal itself. Great ingenuity was exercised in the combination of reducing alloys and substitutes until at last, in the degenerate days of the Dark Ages, alchemists began to dream of a "philosopher's stone"

which should in fact transmute base metal into pure gold thrice re-
fined. The idea was, of course, chimerical, and the outgrowth of that
period of unregenerate mystery. Like most falsehoods, however, this
utterly futile theory held in it the germ of a great truth which was
not to dawn on civilisation for generations after. The transmutation
of the basic elements of nature cannot, we concede, be accomplished,
however much they may be combined in new forms; but with force
itself, how different is the story, for the transmutation of force is a
recognised and, I had almost said, an everyday matter. Indeed, so
far as Nature herself goes, it is a thing not of hourly but of constant
occurrence, and may be studied under the accepted name of the
"correlation of force" and thus we shall see that heat, light, and sound,
different as they seem to us and varying as their sense-demonstra-
tions certainly are, may nevertheless be interchanged, the one into
the other, or "transmuted" almost at the will of the scientist, in spite
of their distinguishing characteristics. Neither time nor inclination
leads one to take up too pedagogic an explanation of the subject here,
nor would it be pertinent to go deeply into such questions as the
direction of the segments of vibrations producing sense-reaction.
Some of these vibrations are longitudinal and some as we know are in
cross section; and these facts are daily turned to the account of
science, but we must pass them by, since they do not directly concern
us. The point to be scored with emphasis is the fact of the absolute

harmony of these forces and the subjection of the laws governing each group to the unified purpose of the whole, as shown by the possibility of this transmutation which goes on every day.

Without spending an unwarranted amount of time on detail, let us accept the truth of the three fundamental laws of gravitation, sound, and light, relative to the intensity and effectiveness of each, and I cannot state these more tersely than has been done previously. [1]

Gravity: The force of gravity varies inversely as the square of the distance through which it is exercised:

Sound: The intensity of sound varies inversely as the square of the distance through which it must pass.

Light: The intensity of light varies inversely as the square of the distance from the luminous body.

That all of these should diminish progressively as the effect recorded is more and more distant from the originating cause is what we should expect and what our daily observation teaches us unconsciously, but that the exact proportion of this diminution should be governed by the same rule in every case is, to say the least, a somewhat startling revelation of the unity of this control which Nature exercises over everything and a singular confirmation of the claim that the harmony of her laws is no specious theory but a hard fact, worthy of study. Here we have three laws governing those forces

[1] *Nature's Harmonic Unity*, page 185.

which are most common to our knowledge, and these three laws are
not merely similar, but are *absolutely identical.* They are not only
identical, but they are, moreover, strictly geometric in their operation.
They are not only identical and geometric, but they are, furthermore,
indisputably subject to those factors which are the constructive base
of the tetragon family, since their elemental relation, gauging the
intensity by the distance, is the square.[1]

For the purpose of ocular demonstration, let us inspect plate
40, which I have prepared for the purpose of making clear exactly
how this triplicate rule works through every second of time and will
continue to work until eternity sets its seal upon all things. It is
hardly necessary to state that the rule in question is not limited in its
truth by the progressive points in the illustration, nor by the three
instances chosen, but is equally true in its operation anywhere and
everywhere, over distances visible only through the microscope and
over spaces unconceived by the human brain. The relationship
between the volume of sound, light, and gravity, and their reduction
as the distance is increased is, however, told with absolute accuracy
by the diagram, and *this relation is invariably one represented by the
square.* If in this plate, we suppose that the attraction of gravitation
be exercised by any body of matter or that sound or light be generated
by any source, first, over a distance represented by the line AD in the

[1] Appendix, Note XV.

third circle of figure one, and that the distance be then increased until

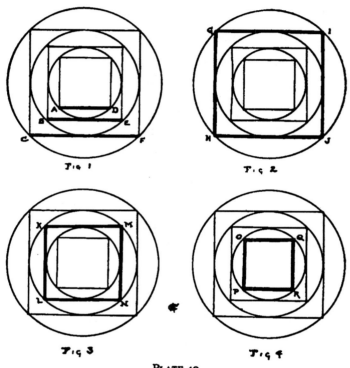

PLATE 40

FORCES COMPARED

A SYMBOLIC DIAGRAM ILLUSTRATING THE PARALLEL BETWEEN THE
FORCES OF LIGHT, SOUND, AND GRAVITATION IN PROPORTION
TO THE DISTANCE OVER WHICH THEY ARE EXERCISED.
FROM *The Great Modules*

it equals BE and finally again increased to CF, then we know positively that the intensity of the gravity, sound, or light will diminish as

the distance increases, in proportion as expressed by the rule, and that, from being equal to the square shown in the circle of figure two at the time when the distance is least, as at AD, it will diminish to the square KM when the distance is as BE, and again be reduced to the dimensions of the square OPQR in circle four of the plate when the distance is increased to equal CF. The point of amazement is reached when we realise that these statements are equally true and this table is equally applicable, whether we speak of gravity, sound, or light. To realise the universality of this application and the overpowering supremacy of this force of gravity, we have but to visualise it as it is: the one only common property of all mankind. The blind see not, the deaf hear not, and for measurable periods we do not even breathe the air; the lame walk not, the dumb talk not, every sense and sensibility may be suspended or lost, but while a particle remains we shall be conscious of weight and subject to the force of gravity which keeps us to the last, circumspectly in our several places and maintains the stars in their ordered course.

SOUND

We have first taken up the subject of gravity because, of all the forces of Nature it is, as we have seen, by far the most universal; and on the same logical principle, the topic of sound should come next, since, while light is more universal than sound, the human anatomy is so constructed that light and its correlatives, colour and form, may be shut out voluntarily. The two latter come to the sense of man only from the direction in which the eye is deliberately cast, while sound assails him from every direction and whether he will or no. Of sound (as of light and gravity) we already know that the intensity varies as the square of the distance from the cause to the effect, and the intensity of sound as it reaches the ear and is heard, depends also on the original loudness (amplitude or wave-width), which we cannot well spare the time to investigate. Since the other factor of intensity, the distance through which the wave must travel, has already been considered in our symbolic tabulation, we have reduced by one the four vital subdivisions which present themselves to the mind in considering the question of sound; intensity, quality, pitch, and combination.

The question of quality moreover is one which, equally interesting though it be, nevertheless presents refinements in research which are little adapted to such a work as the one in hand, or consonant with its necessary brevity, and we shall therefore confine our little hour to the remaining questions of pitch and combination, or harmony, as understood by musicians.

When the blacksmith's boy, idling in front of the wheel-wright's busy shop, whirled a wagon wheel briskly around and thrumed the spokes with a hickory stick in his hand, we remember that we noticed a number of things. When the wheel went slowly, the result was a mere racket, which the boy was invited to stop at once. Whirling the wheel faster and faster, the irritating noise became a musical note, the pitch of which depended on the size of the felloes and spokes and the rapidity of motion. If we gave the matter any thought, we realised that these conditions producing pitch were capable of four composite results; the sound might either be loud and high, loud and low, soft and high, or soft and low, depending on whether the blows which were the sound-impulse were strong and fast, strong and slow, weak and fast, or weak and slow. Let us then keep constantly in mind that the intensity of the sound which is, as we have said, measured by the wave-width or amplitude, depends on the strength of the blow or impulse, while the pitch depends entirely upon the speed of vibration. It is well also to recognise the fact that scientific sounds exist continually to which the human ear is not attuned and which pass us by as do the ultra-violet and infra-red colour waves, which, quite invisible to the human eye, work in our laboratories daily, taking X-ray photographs on plates sensitised to see what escapes the vision of mankind.

It will not suffice, in a work devoted to proportions in beauty, to treat sound as mere noise. If we are to study sound from the standpoint of beauty we cannot escape the subject of music as a general basis, since that is the great sound-art, and while it would be trite to say that the great majority of people would decry the very idea that the choice of a musical scale or the selection of chords in a composition were governed by any mathematical rules, and would stoutly maintain that mathematics would be the death of artistic sense, yet if one goes into the matter fundamentally it is quickly seen that every accepted law of musical composition and the very structure of the diatonic scale itself is based on rules which guide, consciously or unconsciously, every acceptable production. The most ignorant and illiterate booby may learn, with the aid of a good eye and sensitive touch, to play a presentable game of billiards; yet never in the whole course of his practice will he make a good shot unscientifically. If the table be true, the balls round, the cues in order, such a thing as an accidental shot is impossible, chance being practically eliminated. The only element of accident lies wholly within the player, for if the shot brings the balls where they should be, it is because the correct power, direction, and "English" were in the stroke, no matter how awkward it may seemingly have been delivered. A beautiful play must, however unconsciously, be played with mathematical perfection, else it would have been a miss. In music likewise, deny it as we may, yet in order to produce the result desired, we are compelled to be mathematical and scientific whether we will or no, and consequently the earlier we undertake the proper study of the science of sound, the more surely shall we achieve success. Let us see if this cannot be illustrated.

Were we suddenly born into a new world where music was unknown, could we construct a musical scale based on the declared preference of a majority of the people for one set of notes as against another? And if we did so, should we not, after all, be taking unconscious advantage of the facts which have been scientifically established, even though we failed to acknowledge it to our inmost hearts? Let us readily admit that savage nations gather together and make weird sounds unrelated to the diatonic scale as recognised by the civilised world; but in venturing to call this music, let us tread softly, remembering that with savages, and with most orientals, ceremonial music has largely to do with mysticism, with legendary habit, with awe, fear, mimicry, spells, narcotics, and with practically everything except beauty. Choice, originality, pleasure, creative aspiration, genius, talent, have small place in this system which has religious exhilaration and fanaticism for its father and mother, habit for its cradle, and heredity as nurse-maid, and is beautiful only by accident and in rare instances.

Looking back over the world's history, can we find ever a man who lived before music had theories either to bind or loose it, a man with the wit to investigate it and set down such rules and laws as seemed to him to lead to beauty in sound? Strange to say, yes, once was there such a man, with the wit and the mind and the forethought to make copious notes of what he learned about beauty. I need not tell you that his name was Pythagoras, the Greek, who studied the one-stringed lute or Æolian harp, singing in the breeze; and after much experiment and years of study, he enunciated a law of musical pitch which we can illustrate by referring to plate 41, and which law has never been disproved.

Dividing his string into halves, as at C in figure two of plate 41 by placing a bridge under this node, he found that the halves produced the same note, and that they sounded agreeably together, and particularly agreeable when struck at the same time with a second string as in figure one which gave the same tone as the whole string, undivided. Well might these things be true, since the ends of the divided string, having equal rapidity of vibration, sounded notes in unison, while the ends of the halved string gave out notes exactly an octave higher than that of the whole cord sounded alone. A little later we shall try to see if there were no scientific reason why these things were so, but this may safely rest a moment, since Pythagoras knew nothing of the reasons, merely recognising the facts, and keeping an impatient world on its tiptoes in anticipation all these centuries to find out whether he was guessing in the dark or whether, on the contrary, there should at last develop a reason. Returning for a moment to Pythagoras whom we left rather unceremoniously, we find him engaged in dividing his cord into two such portions as that the longer should be twice the shorter, as in figure three of the plate, at the division at E. Sounding these, the tones were, he declared, again sources of pleasure.

And again, well might he say so, since, as compared with the note of the longer, the shorter end sounded the octave. Dividing again, so that the two ends should have the relation of two to three, as at the point M in figure five, the sounds, equally agreeable, were those we now

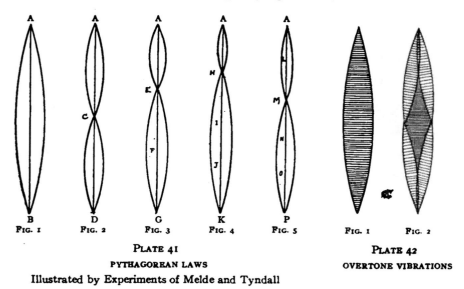

FIG. 1   FIG. 2   FIG. 3   FIG. 4   FIG. 5   FIG. 1   FIG. 2

PLATE 41   PLATE 42

PYTHAGOREAN LAWS   OVERTONE VIBRATIONS

Illustrated by Experiments of Melde and Tyndall

recognise as the tonic and dominant. After much such experiment, Pythagoras deduced his rule which the world accepted long in advance of any assignable reason based upon a scientific theory. The rule, reduced to simplicity, holds that "The simpler are the ratios of the two segments into which a cord is divided, the more perfect is the harmony of the notes produced." And it was true. And because, all unbeknown to Pythagoras, a reason existed for it, so it remains as true today as it was when the world was young.

Countless generations passed before anyone discovered the various facts which enable us to guess at a reason why he was right. Science eventually developed the wave theories to account for sound, and finally accepted a similar theory in regard to light and the world advanced to the point that so many theories had been surrounded by facts, hard and cold, that a number of these could be raised from their classification of mere theories, the "*quod erat demonstrandum*" of doubt erased, and filed in the archives of law immutable.

It is generally easier to accept a statement proved to the eye than in any other way, and the demonstrations regarding these sound waves as created by cords might, had we the time, be beautifully shown by the experiments of Melde, as diagrammed in plate 41 to which we have been referring. A white silk cord, made to vibrate in a direct light, will sound as a whole until the tension at the end is sufficiently increased when, without ceasing to vibrate, it will divide its segments into two, as shown in figure two, then into three, as in figure three, and so on until perhaps twenty segments are sounding their notes at once from the same string, and all visible to the eye. Sometimes, indeed, the main cord can be made to continue its own vibration as a whole, sounding the tonic, while, at the same time it will vibrate separately in octave segments, as illustrated in plate 42, sounding thus the "harmonics" or "overtones" on which certain musical effects depend.

Having led up to the state of present knowledge, let us see if we can now ascribe any reason for the pleasurable sensation derived from the sounding of the cord-segments as divided by Pythagoras.

Even a very slight knowledge of psychology will show us that the human mind receives a pleasant stimulus in observing the actual occurrence of that which it has anticipated, for which reason an appreciation of poetry is almost universal. The rhythm of the metre excites the expectation, as does the anticipation of the succeeding rhyme. So, again, it is natural that the rhythm of music, the undulations of the ocean, the swaying of the dance, the curving flight of our goldfinch, call up responsive emotion. Upon this we may postulate the explanation of many of man's most familiar pleasures.

If, now, it be true, as obviously it is, that the human mind is so constructed that it enjoys rhythm and unity, then it would be logical to suppose that two notes having the greatest number of characteristics in common would present the greatest unity and would be correspondingly pleasing. Comparing this rule deduced from science with the ancient conclusions of Pythagoras, and again with the diagram which I have endeavoured to make illustrative of the subject without requiring cumbersome explanations, and which is shown as plate 43,[1]

[1] Appendix, Note XVI.   Tension and weight must remain unchanged.

we find that the tonic and octave, which Pythagoras obtained by
dividing his cord into segments such that the one was twice the other,
were produced by vibrations exactly twice as fast in the one case as
in the other, that being the ratio which exact science sets for any two
notes which are octaves. Pythagoras found, you will recollect, that
the simplest ratios produced the most agreeable harmonies, and here,
at the first experiment, we find that the simplest ratio produces the
one in which the vibrations and their corresponding nodes or quiet
zones are so timed as to coincide most frequently, exactly as we had
presupposed. Being a trifle more graphic, I may say in other words,
that every second sound wave of the upper note of these two was
exactly timed to and coincided absolutely with a vibration of the
lower, and this will be recognised as a matter of no small moment when
it is comprehended that in an average case, such as C^2 and its octave,
the enormous number of five hundred and twenty-eight vibrations
would coincide *in every second*, and that in every second, the same
number of nodes or quiet places would coincide, as well. Euler and
Helmholtz both have advanced highly scientific and complex explanations for the undeniable fact that concurrent octaves are more
agreeable to the ear than, for example, concurrent sevenths in which
nearly an equal number of opposed vibrations occur; but it would
seem that no great surprise is caused in assuming the logical at-
titude that the absence of something over five hundred clashing

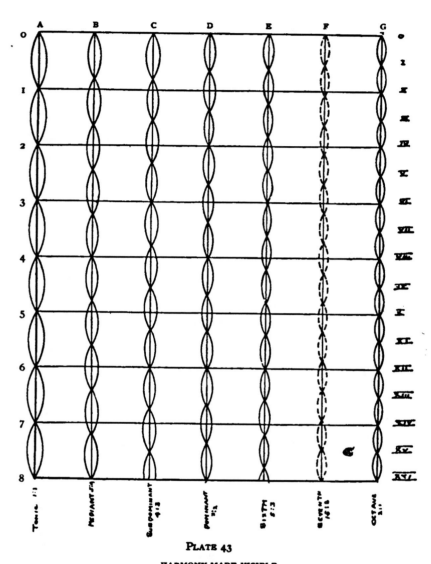

PLATE 43

HARMONY MADE VISIBLE

Symbolic tabulation of vibration.   Taken from *The Great Modules*

vibrations of sound per second might do much toward making the octave an agreeable sound. To test this, however, let us proceed to Pythagoras's second experiment, where we see that by division of his ratios into 3 : 2, the shorter string emits the dominant in relation to the tonic of the longer. Scientific inspection then presents us with the fact that the coincidence of vibration and quiet in this case is one in three, and again we see a logical reason for the acceptability of the sounds in harmony.

Proceeding on this plan we find that we have quickly constructed what is known as the "common chord" which is the basis of all harmony, and in which the vibrations and peaceful nodes are concurrent with such frequency as to smooth away all dissonance. This chord then is agreeable, not because we choose to think it so, and not because good musicians say that it should be so, and not because we have heard it all our lives, but simply and only because it is based on the constructive factors which make it so whether one listens with pleasure or is one of the unfortunately musically deaf persons whom we occasionally meet.

Now, at the risk of losing a moment's time, let us examine these musical notes which evidently are the chosen of the civilised world for some good and sufficient reason, spite all of the customary objections to the mingling of reason and mathematics with inspirational subjects, and see how their relations with each other bear out the

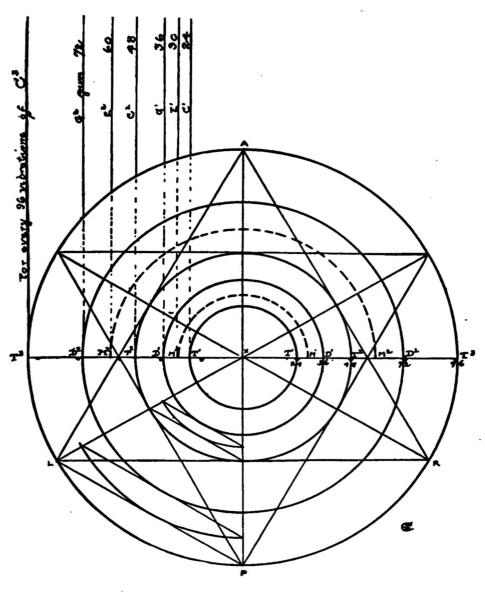

PLATE 44

GEOMETRIC DIAGRAM OF PITCH INTERVALS

115

theory which I have propounded, that all of these demonstrations of force are geometrical in their action, and that in a large majority of cases their demonstration will disclose that their basis is the tetragon family, with the hexagon looming large. We have already seen what part the hexagon plays in the accurate measurement of the planetary system which we know is founded on the gravitational laws. Now let us make an experiment on that section of sound which we call music (*i.e.*, the part of sound which we select as being "beautiful"). The result is shown in plate 44, wherein we find the notes of the diatonic scale depicted with their vibratory relations in a diagram of progressive hexagons and which is repeated here from a former work as being necessary to continuity of the study. As in the case of the astronomical chart in which the hexagon occurred, it would be well to caution the reader that the illustration here introduced is intended only *as* an illustration, the actual calculation being made by logarithmic triangulation, and correct to a point infinitely beyond the possible capacity of a sheet of paper and a pencil, correct indeed, beyond the use of a microscope to disclose.[1]

The interesting mathematical accuracy with which these statements are true can only be disclosed by recourse to the dry processes of calculation which probably would not interest the reader but which is demonstrable nevertheless; but if from what I have said it has been

[1] *See* Appendix, Note XVII.

made clear that the laws of pitch are geometric and that they are persistently similar to those which govern outward form under the influence of gravity, my object will have been attained.

It is not, however, impossible to cajole Nature into making some of her own diagrams on the interesting subjects which we have under our observation, and it would seem that if sound waves can thus be induced to write their story so that it is visible to the eye, surely the argument will be well-nigh unanswerable. For this purpose, we will undertake in plate 45 several of the Chladni experiments, such as were shown in great variety by Tyndall, by clamping glass plates in the centre and scattering fine sand over the surface. If then, sound waves be set in motion by drawing a violin bow lightly across the edge, the grains of sand will be set into violent motion and it will be found that they will dance gaily over the surface and find a resting place on those portions of the plate where the vibration is least severe. The termination of all wave action will find the plate patterned with sand, the nodes being covered and the ventral segments, where action was continuous, being bare. The pattern thus formed may be varied by the experimenter at will by damping one or more spots on the edge of the plate, thus causing intervening nodes, which will repeat themselves geometrically through the course of the vibration at other correlative points, so that, whatever be the position of the damped node, the diagram of the sand at rest will invariably be found perfectly geometric, with straight lines and curves at perfectly balanced distances, and showing a marked similarity of pattern to those disclosed in the crystal and diatom and other formations built up under the influence of force.

PLATE 45
CHLADNI'S EXPERIMENTS

It might, perhaps, be claimed with seeming justice that by selecting a square plate the experimenter had to some extent forced Nature to choose tetragonal and octagonal forms for her patterns: but what will be the answer when it is shown that these same conditions persist with equal pertinacity even when the plates be round, as shown in plate 46: and further, that the bubbles in round glass vessels may be made to vibrate in the same way, forming patterns for which this illustration might be taken as the reproduction, so alike are they. In short, we may understand that it is almost impossible to produce any other class of arrangement, however different may be the beautiful detail, as shown on the face of the snow crystal.

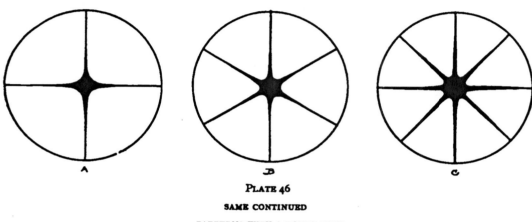

PLATE 46

SAME CONTINUED

PATTERNS WITH A ROUND DISK

Let us even go a step further and examine the vibrations of a bell as shown in diagram 47, where we see that the sound waves set up actual motion in the walls of the bell and that these cross at four nodes forming a perfect square. Here, certainly, Nature has had full sway to create a pattern after her own sweet will. Why then did she not choose the magic seven or any other number of divisions than this constant repetition of the four which we have so frequently observed in actions of force.

I may add that if there should be any lingering feeling that these sound waves do not set up an actual physical motion in the atoms constituting the walls of the bell, a further experiment is possible. If a slender glass tube be subjected to the influence of sound waves, it may be shivered into exact fragments at the instant that the pitch

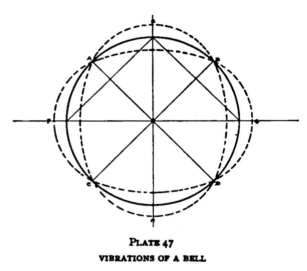

PLATE 47

VIBRATIONS OF A BELL

reaches the "note" of the tube, and if pyrotechnics were desirable, a cannon might easily be shot off by the addition of a simple mechanism operated by a properly attuned sound wave. Indeed, in recent war days, we have been hearing any number of accounts of the explosions thus sympathetically caused, if report be true, at distant points, by the use of properly keyed wave lengths from established stations.

LIGHT

If we shall spare less space in the treatment of the subject of light than has been expended in examining sound, it is merely because the subjects are in many ways so akin that what has been said in regard to the one need not be repeated regarding the other. Sound, it must be understood, fills the atmospheric universe and as has been said, is not confined to those waves which beat within the limited capacity of the human ear. In the same way, colour and light exist where no human eye detects them, the retina being attuned only to those which fall within the spectrum, being visible only as between the lowest reds and the highest violets. Turning again to this question of rapidity, it is not without interest to note that, judged by the speed of vibration, the whole gamut of visibility is contained within the compass of one colour octave. I do not use this expression as a mere fanciful one, but as denoting in hard and scientific calculation, the vibratory relation of the shortest visible ray, the violet, to the longest one, the red,—a relation which is exactly double in speed. We know that if a ray become faster and shorter than any we can see, we recognise it by scientific experiment as "ultra-violet": we know it exists, we use it daily, we have felt it burn us, we have seen its mark on silvered photographic plates, but no one has ever seen it, nor by direct observation, will it ever be seen. The slow or infra-red rays, we admit, also surround us and have their constant influence on vegetation and serve the daily needs of Dame Nature perhaps as usefully as the rays upon which we count for our groping way through life.

I have at numerous points called attention to the fact that the recorded evidences of gravity, sound, and light are tetragonal in so many cases as to refute all hasty denial, and if I be permitted one more illustration of the subject it may, perhaps, be possible to "put it all under one roof," as the saying goes. Let us revert to our case of the bell, and see what can be gathered from watching, listening, and noting. The vibrations, we note, are causing the very shape of the bell itself to change in a direct relation to the square, despite its circular form. This we know from all authorities and from the illustration already examined. The swinging of the wheel and the bell is dependent altogether upon gravity, without which they might be pulled one way but would never come back. Gravity, we have seen, operates on the bell in a strict accordance with the law of the square. We listen to the sounds produced, which are carried to our ears by the vibrational laws likewise tetragonal in their entire make up. We also watch the operation of ringing or tolling by vision brought to us by the light waves, controlled, as are all of the other means mentioned, by the laws which we have been studying. Does all of this unity convey no conclusion to the mind?

It is doubtless time to put this portion of our subject away from us, and it behooves one to summarise slightly between untouched aspects of the similarity between the laws of light and sound before calling a dead halt.

Concerning the transmission of sound and light to points distant from the source, we may dismiss the comparison from further study, since the laws have been seen to be identical. The similarity, however, does not terminate with the question of transmission, but goes on and on, practically as long as our study continues. We have seen, for instance, that the pitch of sound depends on the rapidity of vibration. So, also, the colour of light depends on this same rapidity of vibration. Remembering that dissimilarity of colour means, in effect, visibility, and we shall more nearly appreciate the importance of all this, for, without nicely balanced variance of colour, even form would be nearly invisible, unless outlined directly against a strong light, and the whole system of war camouflage has been built up around the knowledge of such facts as these. Remember colour as being only the residuum, so to speak, of unabsorbed rays of light. What we speak of as red is, in fact, only that part of the unbroken white ray which has been turned back, reflected, or refracted, by some object which, according to its nature, swallows up the balance and hands us what it does not need.

Just as the harmony of combined sounds has been shown, I think, conclusively, to depend on combinations in which the vibratory waves and nodes are most consonant and have the most in common, so colour-harmony depends on a similar consonance. We have found that in sound, agreeable chords were formed of notes vibrating at common periods, and an examination of these will disclose the fact that in wave-value, harmonic notes were *never near neighbours*. The octave, representing the entire sound gamut mathematically, resounds so agreeably that whole choruses are composed to be performed in unison, or octaves. The next most agreeable combinations, third and tonic and fifth and tonic, are spaced nearly equally in the vibratory scale; and, desiring a combination of rough dissonance, who does not at once hit upon joining the seventh and octave, or the dominant and sub-dominant, as embodying the worst that the key-board presents? The same is precisely true of colour. The agreeable common chord of light is composed of those colours nearly equally spaced in the spectrum, and these are found harmonic, while those which are the nearest neighbours in vibration, such as two shades of green, or two related reds, or red and pink, are, by public consent, voted impossible or worse.[1]

I might go on indefinitely with illustrations taken from the great free book, but enough has been developed, one would think, to show beyond peradventure of a doubt, the homogeneity of the laws govern-

[1] Appendix, Note XVIII.

ing matter with those controlling force, and to indicate the persistence, to say the least, with which Nature adopts the forms of the tetragon family when she wishes to express herself through the action of these invisible agents.

In concluding the arguments formed along the lines of this chapter, I would put a few pointed questions to the reader for his self-searching.

We know that certain varieties of vegetable life, flowers and the like, are habitually clothed in green. This means, we understand, that they are thus furnished with an outside sheath or husk or bark or skin, which absorbs certain light rays and rejects those others which come to our eyes as colour. I will pay you the compliment, reader, of supposing that you do not believe that this is all accident, nor that each case is an exception, but that Nature has a purpose in it all. Am I right? Admitting, then, a purpose, do you believe that the purpose differs each time, or is steadfast and always the same; and that the colour of the flower is frequently the result of its needs, and, so to speak, prescribed by this great doctor? Granting that this is done for a purpose and that the purpose is steadfast and has rule and law behind it, do you believe that it is the same in all cases where the facts are the same? If that be granted, and if we admit, as admit we must, that colour is a pure matter of mathematics, or vibratory speed and length, do you believe that mathematical rules (or perhaps I should say rules which we visualise as mathematics) apply to colour and gravity but not to forms and shapes? Or if these forms are controlled by mathematical rules, that these shapes are assumed as the result of either accident or without a purpose? A well-known writer has recently said that no purpose could be ascribed to Nature from her forms nor could it be thought that she had any intention as gathered from her use of one configuration as against another. Do you believe anything so scandalous of her? In other words, do you believe, as I asked in the introduction, that there is a reason for making certain lilies always white but no reason for making the same blossoms always six-cornered? If you believe that there is reason in the mathematical government of colours, and moreover, that the rules concerning this class are uniform, and that there is some rule as to shape, why is not that rule uniform also? If you believe that Nature has these uniform rules which govern form, motion, colour, and sound (the fundaments of all beauty) and that these rules are mathematical, as can scarcely be denied, do you then believe that beauty and mathematics and geometry and reason can live together in peace and amity? Indeed, do you believe that beauty can exist or survive except with reason in her favour? We may not know at all why or how we live and move and have our being, but the why and the how must accord nevertheless to the rules or behold, we are as dead as the thirty centuries. With beauty, I contend it is not different. Committed to the theory that beauty is purposeless, aimless, with rhyme perhaps but certainly without reason, insulted equally by laws and by measurements, and all research is not only lost but becomes a direct impertinence. Admit that, in spite of the latitude and necessity of genius, reason must support all beauty, even if the reason takes unattractive mathematical or scientific form, and we have a warrant for investigation and a fair hope of reward. If we are agreed so far on these points, then let us go hand in hand along the path, for perchance we may discover something worth while. If we do not agree, then let us part, for we need treatment at the hands of different oculists.

CHAPTER V

ASYMMETRY AND VARIETY[1]

AN ANTIDOTE FOR SYMMETROPHOBIA

THE ancient Egyptians and, to some extent, the artistic and perhaps no less ancient Japanese, dreaded in their creations what they felt to be the taint of symmetry as they dreaded only the plague. It is not necessary that we should altogether agree with them in this in order to understand that one has not far to go in such a study as ours, before realising that the number of subjects of interest which cannot be conventionalised, cannot easily be surrounded by polygons nor subjected to the geometrical measurements or to analyses such as we have so far sketched, far outnumber those which submit themselves readily to these methods. Other means therefore have to be devised for the examination of these less manageable subjects and we shall treat them briefly in this chapter both for convenience' sake and because many varying classes may be found to belong, on inspection, to the same natural or geometric family.

The beauty of all of these forms has many times been keenly felt

[1] From *The Great Modules*, C. Arthur Coan, 1914.

128

when, perhaps, it could scarcely be expressed. Such a marvellous brain as that of Leonardo could conceive the perfectly correct idea that the wing-tips of flying birds formed lines which were spiral in their completed whole; and this stood, like the sound theories of Pythagoras, as a charming and useless brain-child for several hundred years until, in Leonardo's case, the kinematograph came to the rescue and proved that he was perfectly accurate in his surmise. Every great mathematician, every great artist, every great architect, in the past generations has felt the urge of these varied curves which are not circles; and many have given invaluable time to their analysis, nor could the results be packed into a mere chapter. Space forbids a review of these previous studies *in extenso*. They are, nevertheless, open to all of the serious minded: and I would guard against the thought that any attempt has been made to catalogue or recite any considerable portion of what has been said concerning these beauties of form and attendant colour which await the searcher.

In these many forms of non-circular curves, then, which will be observed to divide themselves into various families akin to our list, we shall find ellipses, segments based on the ideal angle, catenary curves, graphic indices, eccentrics, and spirals without regard to their several geometric values or their family relations. Asymmetric as they generally are, we shall see their many beauties and in some instances we shall take the time to analyse them, though this will not

9

always be either practicable or profitable. If something must be left in life to the imagination, so, after proper groundwork, must something be constantly left to the student.

There is necessarily a certain amount of latitude in the use of such terms as symmetry and asymmetry, even if by symmetry we mean an exact repetition of one part by another. Here every element of form on the one hand would have an exact counterpart on the other, each side paired by its twin, reversed in order, detail, and position as if reflected in a mirror,—as like as the Twinnes of Hippocrates, which, you will recollect, were as like as two pease in a pod. Disregarding certain minor differences, the outward semblance of the human form, for example, is decidedly symmetrical. Interiorly, on the contrary, it is very much otherwise, with only one heart and that on one side; with some organs functioning in pairs and some without a mate, and with nerves, like little electric bell wires, clinging first here and then there to complete the circuit required in the fulfilment of their high office. The asymmetrical things in this world greatly outnumber the symmetrical.

Let us not, however, fall into the error of supposing that, because things asymmetrical cannot readily be conventionalised, they are therefore without law and order. Asymmetry affords us many pleasures of beauty denied by the more staid forms of symmetry, and furnishes us that variety which Cowper says is "the very spice of life, that gives it all its flavour," but to teach this as being a freedom from law would be to preach anarchy—the very antipodes of that variety-filled but well-regulated Nature

"Where order in variety we see
　　And where, though all things differ, all agree."

CATENARY CURVES[1]

Amongst all of the free curves of Nature, one of the commonest is the catenary, which is formed through the agency of gravitation, which we perhaps better comprehend now with its pervading presence, the most universal in its application of all the forces discovered by mankind. I would not have it understood that all catenary curves are formed by gravity, nor, indeed, that gravity forms no curves other than these, for neither conclusion would be true, but it is nevertheless true that the study of this form necessarily presupposes an understanding of the force which holds the stars in the sky, which power we recognise as gravity.

As a mere laboratory or mathematical conclusion, even without the demonstrations found on every hand, one might correctly assume that so effective a force, working by itself, would produce straight

[1] From *The Great Modules*, 1914.

lines, and that, acting in opposition to counter-forces and restraints, would produce curved lines. Opening her great book, we find that every page is inscribed with these results in curves, and if Nature seems to abhor straight lines, even as she does a vacuum, it is merely because the force of gravity so seldom finds scope for demonstrations uninfluenced by other causes.

Newton's apple, falling directly from the tree to the ground, seemed to draw a straight line from branch to sod, but careful examination would unerringly prove that the diminution of eastward motion of the earth and other complications, once the apple was released, had imparted a parabolic twist which, slight as its hold could be in the infinitesimal time needed for the fall, yet certainly it deflected the sphere from that perfect vertical which it seemed to describe.[1]

No one who has for a moment glanced at a chain caught at both ends and swinging its loose bight in the sunshine ever failed to note the graceful curves formed in every motion. These catenary curves are among the freest examples of the influence of gravity and, while none of them conform to the lines of the circle, differing from each other according as the distance at which the ends are made fast, they are, perhaps for that very reason, hard to match for their beauty and grace, and Ruskin's line of beauty, the "infinite line, which does not

[1] Appendix, Notes XIX and XXXIV.

return upon itself," to which reference has already been made, applies almost as directly to the catenary as to the spirals. Various forms of this curve are illustrated in plate 48, and an inspection of plates 15 and 16 will show there any number of these catenary curves engraved on the face of the snow crystals which are the object of those illustrations.

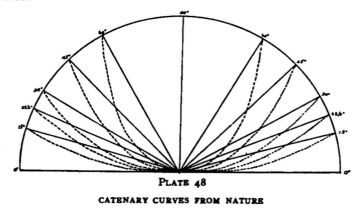

PLATE 48
CATENARY CURVES FROM NATURE

Strictly speaking, of course, we recognise the fact that a catenary curve, geometrically, is any curve of a perfectly flexible, infinitely fine cord, when at rest under the influence of force, while the common catenary is what the catenary becomes when the forces are parallel and proportional to the length of the cord, as in the case of a heavy cord of uniform weight under the influence of gravitation. The practical use in everyday scientific life of the catenary curve comes from the understanding of the fact that this form lends itself, as one of

Nature's agents, to the carrying of weights as well as to a smooth and unfrictional passage through air and water. Hence both the bridge builder and the boat designer are entirely familiar with its nature and utilitarian purposes, whatever they may think as to its inspiring beauty.

The bridge builder and the boat designer, however, would be quite lost if they were obliged to trace the arcs which they wished to

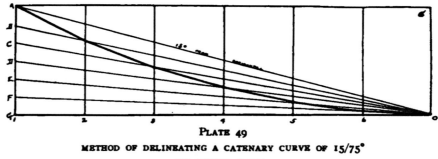

PLATE 49

METHOD OF DELINEATING A CATENARY CURVE OF 15/75°

BY VERSED SINES

test, from actual chains hung in mid-air. Like most beautiful things found in Nature, once man sees their use, he tames them, brings them into his home or his shop, and finally produces them by synthetic processes. Even the catenary curve may thus be built up synthetically (but perhaps not, alas, very sympathetically) with nothing more romantic than a pencil and paper, a ruler and a modicum of scientific knowledge. Suppose we build one to see how it works. Draw first a rectangle having, between its base and its perpendicular, the propor-

tions in which we wish to form our catenary curve. Divide the base
into any number of points and the vertical into the same number:

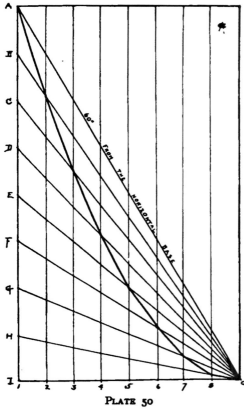

PLATE 50

AN ENGINEER'S DRAFTED DELINEATION OF A CATENARY CURVE OF 60°
BY VERSED SINES

the greater the number, the greater will be the accuracy of the resulting curve. Then from the corner of the base at which the desired

angle has been created, as, for example, 15° at the corner O, plate 49 draw straight lines to the points marked on the vertical and the intersections of these diagonals with the other verticals will mark the points cut by the desired catenary which can then be constructed, or delineated, by merely connecting the indicated points with chords as shown in the diagram.[1]

An upright example, delineating a catenary curve of 60° by this method is also added in plate 50, further to exemplify the principle, and now that we understand a little more about these interesting curves in which Nature indulges so frequently, let us look through our catalogue of Nature's Treasury and see whether we have not been dealing unconsciously with catenary curves all of our lives. Here, for example, is a sketch, taken from an instantaneous photograph of a noted diver making a back dive. Watch every line of the body as the supple muscles form their great arc in plate 51, forming catenaries without limit.

And again see the effect of gravity in forming leaves, both as to their contours, veins, and serrated edges in plates 52 and 53.

Were the above not enough to carry conviction of the universality and beauty of these lines, we could add numberless others but a few will suffice, in which the attention of the reader is invited, first, to the beautiful group of javelin throwers, every athlete bending to his fixed task and denoting the successful effort of the art of a day long

[1] Appendix, Note XX.

since past to depict motion in its various stages and doing so with

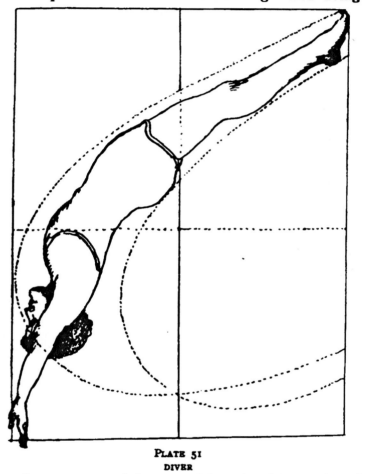

PLATE 51
DIVER

great general accuracy and beauty although without the aid of the kinematograph.

It is not, perhaps, often, that we find a more literal example of
the catenary curve (curve of the chain) than is furnished us on almost

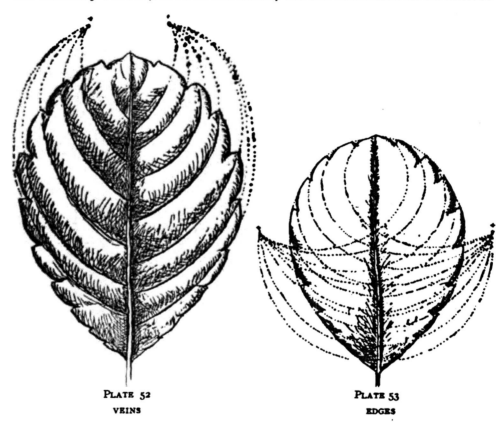

PLATE 52
VEINS

PLATE 53
EDGES

any bright summer morning by the industrious field spider who is
both too wise and too efficient to waste valuable skill and silk in
weaving a net which is to be immediately destroyed by storm. When

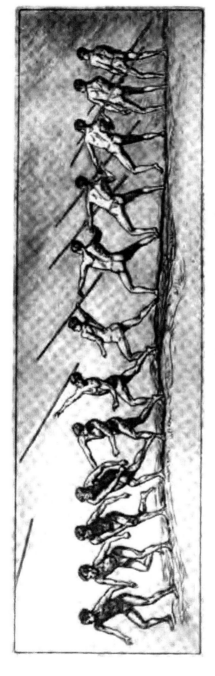

PLATE 54

JAVELIN THROWERS

An old time equivalent of the moving picture. Note the positions of the figures, commencing with the one on the right. In each one, the action is a little farther advanced, and if the direction of the javelins be traced a series of perfect curves will result.

PLATE 55
SPIDER'S WEB (C. V. H. C.)

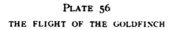

PLATE 56
THE FLIGHT OF THE GOLDFINCH

the fence corners are full of his dangerous entanglements we may feel sure of a fine day, for friend spider weaves to a purpose and believes that the early web catcheth the fat fly. In plate 55 is shown a very direct front view of one of these enticements, with its upper contours sinking into concave loops toward the centre and the lower strands beautifully reversing the process, and drawing for us a diagram of nearly parallel catenaries of singular beauty, and of deadly import to unwary insects still at large. Nor is it only in outward and fixed form that we find fascinating curves in Nature. Watch the goldfinch in plate 56 in his undulant flight. Was ever motion more graceful or soothing or full of cheer? Not swift as a swallow nor yet straight as a hawk, but curvetting coquettishly in delightful little dips which show his rich gold and black to the best possible advantage and expressing these curves in spirited action with a gleam which can scarcely be imitated in a determinate and fixed form.

No one with half an eye has ever passed through life without noting the amazing similarity between mountainous billows and mountains of granite. The evanescent heave and swell, the toss and roll and surge, and the combing of the breakers of the one are duplicated point for point and curve for curve in those age-defying billows of the rolling prairie, the jutting out-crop of the foothills, and the foam-crested peaks in their lonely grandeur. In the one case as in the other, all are the creatures of gravity, and catenary curves are their template and measuring rod. We shall in no wise decrease our interest in the subject if we choose one of our next examples from the Far East and the other from our homeland. Here in plate 57 we have as famous a billow as ever shook its crest or threatened the overthrow and complete destruction of puny man. I need hardly say that it is the "Great Wave of Kanazawa" engraved on wood by that much beloved Japanese, Hokusai, nearly if not quite a hundred years ago. The original cuts are not now common but the illustration before us was made from one of these which fortunately is in our hands. It is a trait of the Japanese artists that they excel in the splendid portrayal of violent action, and this is nowhere better shown than in our clawing tiger of the seas in which graceful catenaries slip through every seething line, whirling up to a final spiral in that over-powering demon, snatching so dramatically at the doomed boats struggling with their human freight below. The giant wave and his six legendary brethren have long since passed along the sands of time, but not so that gallant, curving crest as set by the master's brush and graver for us to compare with the waves of stone.

Last, going back to the ages uncounted, we see in the catenary curves of the old Arizona Needles of the Gila River country, another symbol, older than history, and written when the earth-crust was molten slag, fused with the heat of creation's unquenched fires, but

PLATE 57
THE GREAT WAVE OF KANAZAWA
(Hokusai)

PLATE 58
MOUNTAINS OF THE GILA RIVER COUNTRY

formed into enduring mountains by these laws of gravity which were as fixed then as they are immutable in the present.

ELLIPSES AND THE LIKE

Distinguishing between those curves which turn always at a fixed distance from a focus or centre and those which are never continuously at the same focal distance, is to distinguish between the true circle and all of those other curves which go to make life interesting. The difference is, of course, familiar to us, but the examination of the co-ordinates is a matter difficult to any but the mathematician. This, however, need not debar us from a glance at a number of the points which are impressed upon us in our daily rounds, and of all of these non-circular figures, none have a stronger influence upon our human lives than the ellipse.

When we are able to interchange ideas, if not to clasp hands, across space with the Martians, perhaps they will be found able to tell us why Nature so frequently chooses circular shapes to outline the forms of a fixed or semi-fixed character, while she clings so confidently to the ellipse in her mighty demonstrations of force. Perhaps the Martians know. We do not. Why does the general shape of the circle outline innumerable organic and inorganic objects, from the capitulum of the lowly and humble sunflower all the way to the great

Sun himself,[1] and from cosmos as we see it in our gardens and write it with a small *c*, up, for aught we know, to that Cosmos, with a capital, which envelops all the boundaries of our vision? And again, why, having thus utilised circular forms, should this invisible power then swing our Earth and this same Sun and all the other suns of which he is companion, and perhaps swing Cosmos itself, irresistibly around through not-to-be-conceived orbits, always in an ellipse? The mere contemplation of such magnificent consistency inspires a dumb-stricken awe; and we may hazard any number of guesses, we can state any number of the obvious and beneficial results, but of the fundamental why and how of the choice we have as yet no knowledge. It is as I say. Perhaps the Martians may know. We may, nevertheless be profoundly certain that, whatever Ignorance may from time to time lightly guess, Knowledge will be found invariably hand in hand with reason.

Thus in the study of force we are constantly associated with the ellipse, eked out by our mathematical knowledge which assists us in the distinguishing between a parabola and a hyperbola; but we have no inclination to enter the realm of conic sections except in the one case before us and then only so far as to recognise its importance in the search through the great book spread before us. When we come to consider the question of proportional form as applied in art and

[1] Appendix, Note XXI.

architecture, we shall find that the ellipse plays no mean part in form and ornamentation, both ancient and modern. Let us first spend a moment in considering the question of the asymmetry of the ellipse, as this has bearing on the use of this figure in design. Dr. Denman W. Ross shows by illustrations in the process of one of his works[1] that the ellipse may be symmetrical when, as he expresses it, it is "a figure of measure and shape-balance on a centre" as is shown in plate 59,

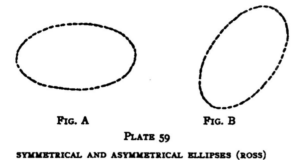

FIG. A   FIG. B

PLATE 59

SYMMETRICAL AND ASYMMETRICAL ELLIPSES (ROSS)

figure A, while it ceases to be symmetrical when it is tilted off the balance as in figure B of the same plate, where, as Dr. Ross naïvely says, "we cannot help feeling that the figure is falling down to the left."

So far as the ellipse is concerned, we can perhaps afford to show, at this point, only one illustration of its use in design. In plate 60 is introduced a reproduction of an ancient Greek loutrophoros, which I

[1] *Theory of Pure Design*, Denman W. Ross (1907).

drew in the Dipylon cemetery at Athens where it was carved in enduring stone long before the day of Christianity and where it still remains
to demonstrate the old ideas. In this slight and fragile pitcher, it will
be seen that all of the commanding lines both of body and handles are
based exclusively on the exact form of the ellipse, and the curves
have been so co-ordinated that an absolute symmetry has been produced as the result, as a glance at the plate will show.

Every engineer will tell us that, even as an ellipse may be symmetrical or asymmetrical, dependent on the position which we force
it to take, so even a perfect circle can be made to have the aspect of
asymmetry if we give it either motion or the appearance of motion, but
force it to revolve or seem to revolve on any point other than its true
centre. Once it becomes eccentric, it assumes the appearance and
attributes of asymmetry. In plate 61, figure A, is depicted a series
of true circles, perfectly symmetrical because set concentrically. The
same circles, revolving on a point not their true and common centre,
as in figure B, become instantly asymmetrical. As a piece of engineering mechanism, the eccentric wheel has numberless uses. As a matter
of decoration, it cannot appear singly, being dependent upon motion,
but several circles may thus be made asymmetric as we see from the
plate, by grouping them about a common point other than their
centres.

Space forbids going further into the intricacies of the various

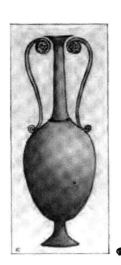

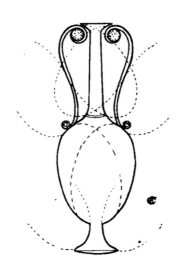

LOUTROPHOROS   ELLIPSE KEY

PLATE 60

ANCIENT GREEK LOUTROPHOROS, SYMMETRICALLY DESIGNED ON AN ELLIPSE

curves which are asymmetrical, except in so far as the spirals of various orders are to be considered. They meet us on every hand: flower-stalks leave out in spirals, the pine cone is a complex mass of them, shells bear their impress, the deer wears them on his head, and man adopts them as among his most varied and pleasurable forms of

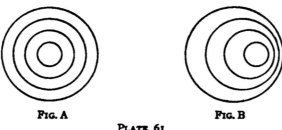

FIG. A   FIG. B

PLATE 61

SYMMETRICAL AND ECCENTRIC CIRCLES

decoration, and his works have been strewn with beautiful designs of which they were the inspiration from the oldest Greek temples to the latest boulevard creation.

SPIRALS

If we lived in that flat country occasionally described by the imaginative, a country having only two dimensions, and thus lacking height, thickness, and depth and we were confined to surfaces only, then chairs and chimneys, mice and mountains, would all tower equally, and the square and triangle, the pentagon and the hexagon would be sufficient to measure nearly everything in reach of the eye. Having been born, on the contrary, into a world of three dimensions, where vertical measurements have as much importance as lateral ones, we come almost immediately upon the need of means to compute and compare them, as we saw in a preceding chapter. The cube is so conceivably akin to the square that the calculation of masses, where these are necessary, presents little to confuse; but where Nature begins to turn and twist in spirals and helices, as she does every day and hour, then we must call in help from outside the processes we have studied elsewhere. Circles, unless eccentrically placed, are, of course, symmetrical, since they measure always the same distance from the centre and produce that repetition which is requisite to strict symmetry. Spirals, on the contrary, wind around the focus like a circle, but, unlike the latter, continually speed farther and farther from the centre. It is true that spirals which are all in one plane occasionally occur—flat spirals—but generally, as they unwind, the elevation changes along with the distance from the centre and we find a summit formed at the centre, or else a helix or cylinder.

There are thus as many kinds of spirals as there are leaves on a tree, but fortunately it will be necessary to study only one or two of these specifically, the generic principles of the subject being sufficient to cover the rest of the ground for our purposes. We shall find in plate 62 six figures showing as many varieties of spirals, two of which

are introduced here because they occur so constantly in natural forms
and in art, and the remaining four because, found less frequently in

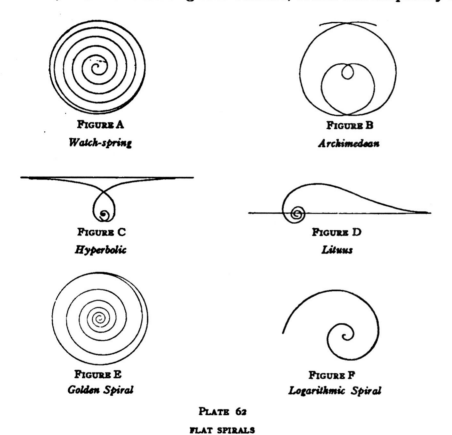

FIGURE A
Watch-spring

FIGURE B
Archimedean

FIGURE C
Hyperbolic

FIGURE D
Lituus

FIGURE E
Golden Spiral

FIGURE F
Logarithmic Spiral

PLATE 62
FLAT SPIRALS

our research, they are nevertheless common to all scientific work and
are perhaps needed to round out the subject.

Doubtless if commanded to draw a spiral and then left to his own devices, the average mortal would first think of something akin to the watch-spring spiral seen in figure A of the plate. This is one offspring of the parabolic form, and the one before us might popularly be differentiated from the others by calling attention to the fact that the distances between the arcs of the coil are always the same, whether the arc be an inner or an outer one. Concerning all of these spirals, further and more technical details are laid down in the appendix notes for the benefit of those who care for them.[1] For those whose bent is other than mathematical, it will be sufficient to mention the heart-shaped outline shown in figure B as representing a spiral studied by Conon the Samian and afterwards by Archimedes, and called after the latter, while figures C and D show forms known as the hyperbolic and the lituus. The form represented in figure E is an interesting one based on an increase of radius in the golden series of extreme and mean proportion so that each coil, in its distance from the centre, plays, so to speak, the part of the lesser in our familiar proportion to its next succeeding outward neighbour which, in turn, plays the corresponding part of greater,[2] and is of the same class as figure F.

The logarithmic or equiangular spiral as shown in figure F of plate 62 occurs more frequently in botany and conchology than any other form, and, since this spiral method has been so well stated by Dr. A.

[1] Appendix, Note XXII.   [2] Appendix, Notes XXII and V, D.

H. Church of Oxford, we can scarcely do better than quote, as was done in *Nature's Harmonic Unity*, from his work on *The Relation of Phyllotaxis to Mechanical Laws*, in which Dr. Church expresses his means of studying this interesting form of spiral. "Describe a large circle," says the author, "then draw, with the same centre, a series of concentric circles, making, with the radii, a meshwork of squares as near as can be judged by the eye; in this circular network of squares arranged in radial series, in geometric progression, all lines which are drawn through the points of intersection in any constant manner are logarithmic spirals, or when drawn in the opposite or reciprocal way, will intersect at all points orthogonally." The spiral desired is then described by connecting the selected points of intersection, as, for instance, every third radius with every fifth circle, as shown in plate 63 or every fifth radius with every eighth circle.

If two spirals be turned, one each way and on the same ratio, as the form marked 1 : 1 in the diagram, the result is symmetrical because balanced on the two sides, but if the right turn be, for example, on the fifth radius and the eighth circle, while the left turn is on the fifth circle and the eighth radius, as is also shown on the diagram, the result is asymmetrical and corresponds to that of many of the five to eight objects as seen in botany. Plate 64 shows the form such a spiral takes in the growth of a sunflower.

Dr. Church says that the spiral construction of helianthus or sunflower is based on the ratio of 34: 55 and may be approximated by the ratios 3: 5 and 5: 8.[1] For a correlating description of this construction we will quote the work referred to in which the author goes on to say that "such a pair of curves (3: 5 and 5: 8) is, then, well within the error or drawing, accurate for a 33 + 55 system, and may be used to map out a spiral orthogonal construction; for practical purposes a pair of curves may be cut out in card, fixed to the paper by a pin through the centre of the circle, and used as a rule. By taking a circle of radius equal to that of the curve pattern, and dividing it into fifty-five and also into thirty-four parts, so that one point may be common to the two sets, and using the curves as a rule to mark fifty-five short curves and thirty-four long ones, the whole circle will be plotted out into a spiral meshwork of squares in orthogonal series corresponding to the parastichies of the sunflower capitulum taken as a type."

In so far as the ideal angle of growth, of which we spoke somewhat at length in the first chapters, takes asymmetrical form, it can scarcely be ignored in this connection. Since, however, its great interest to us lies in connection with its relation to the golden series of extreme and mean ratio, its fuller application will be deferred until a following chapter.

[1] *The Relation of Phyllotaxis to Mechanical Laws.* Compare Mathematical Appendix to *Nature's Harmonic Unity*, page 287.

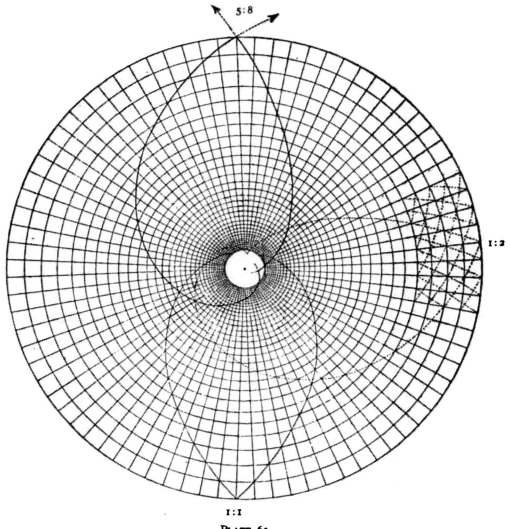

PLATE 63

LOGARITHMIC SPIRAL METHOD
(From Church)

151

It will not escape notice, how akin this method is in ingenuity to that described in plate 49 for the delineation of a catenary curve, and it is interesting to see, further, how Albrecht Dürer, famous as a scientist as he was in art, devised in his *Institutes of Geometry* a method quite in keeping with these two for the depiction of the spiral of an Ionic volute, by first describing a circle divided into any number of segments (twelve in the diagram) and then, one radius being subdivided as with the thread of a screw, drawing short arcs from radius to radius, each arc being one thread farther from the centre than the preceding, until at last the whole radius was worked out. The spiral thus designed, and as shown in plate 65 is, of course, not a logarithmic one, but as in figure A, plate 62, is one with equal spaces between the whorls, and thus lacks that sense of freedom from monotony which is gained by the constant opening out of the thread of the logarithmic spiral, such as the same master hand drew in plate 65, figure B, which, it will be observed, widens constantly as it approaches the perimeter.[1]

It is not at all difficult to see why so few spirals of equally spaced intervals, such as we see in plate 62, figure A, and in Dürer volute are found in Nature, since, were shells, for example, built on this principle, the last portion grown, except as it gains space by rising

[1] *Underweysung der Messung mit dem Zirckel und Richtscheyt, in Linien, Ebnen und Ganzen Corporen*, also Appendix, Note XXIII.

to a central apex, could be of no greater width than the first, and
the opportunity for expansion, so necessary to the life principle,

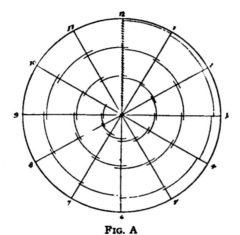

FIG. A

METHOD OF DRAWING IONIC VOLUTE
From Dürer's Underweysung der Messung

FIG. B
LOGARITHMIC SPIRAL
(Dürer)

PLATE 65

would be impossible and life itself would, frequently in the end, be
crushed out. Only in some such form as the logarithmic spiral,

where expansion goes on contemporaneously with progress from
the centre, can Nature generally find room for that enlargement
which is one of her constant features.

Looking, for example, at many of the illustrations, both of botany
and conchology, how clear it is that the expansion in the size of the units
of growth is generally constant, each ring larger than the preceding, until the maximum is reached in the perimeter. Compare this idea, then,
with the possibilities of the same flowers or shells if Nature attempted
to compress them into such a spiral as that drawn by Dürer for his
Ionic volute, instead of the one in which he indicated the logarithmic
order, and we see at once that either the later rows would be the same
size as the earlier ones (in which case the flower would fail both in its
function and in its circular shape) or else the later growth would be
completely strangled.

It is true that natural propagation is seldom in perfect planes,
but examples can nevertheless be economically studied directly from
above with the aid of the flat spirals, as we have seen. Pursuant to
the method of Church, which has recently been followed by so many
other writers, let us examine three plates taken from *Nature's Harmonic Unity* showing the interesting spiral formations of conifers.
Plate 66 gives us the cone of the white pine (Pinus strobus), the yellow
pine is shown in plate 67 and, turning over, we find the Oregon pine
cone on plate 72. These have all been circumstantially described in

PLATE 64
SUNFLOWER CAPITULUM

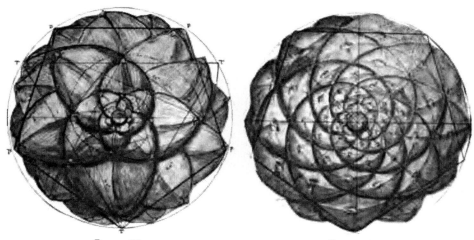

PLATE 66
WHITE PINE CONE

PLATE 67
YELLOW PINE CONE

the former work and space forbids again going deeply into the subject, concerning which it may be deemed sufficient to make the argument a connected one if we merely call attention to the fact that the pips of Pinus strobus will all be found to be grouped along the spirals of the three to five order, which is the simplest shown by any of the conifers; while yellow pine, it will be noted, chooses a form slightly more intricate, being based on spirals of five to eight units, which is a ratio found with extreme frequency. In the Oregon pine we find this principle carried to a still more complex design, this conifer taking as its module the ratio of eight to thirteen, as shown in the illustration.

In all of these it will be noted that the pips, being units capable of individual numbering as completed wholes, bear their relations and ratios in accordance with that integral parallel to the golden series of extreme and mean ratio, the Fibonacci, as explained in the first chapter; and these units of division, constantly capable of enlargement and incapable of comparison by the integral system (since their sizes are matter of constant change) are related to each other by that elastic system, the extreme and mean ratio in all its continuity and perfection, which gives no account to completion nor incompletion, takes no measure of wholes nor fractions, but expands and contracts like a rubber band, always bearing the same relations between its parts, but never the same in itself as was said in the correlating description of this class of seed vessels in the former work. Wherever one goes, whatever one studies or stumbles over, but adds to this constant conviction so strongly expressed in our previous research as to breadth and depth and fulness of the application of this great measure, which led to its adoption as one of the great modules.[1]

Earlier in these pages we have referred to the marvellous pertinacity with which each of the coniferæ adhered to its own allotted form in the matter of needle-bearing, the white pine showing these in clusters of five, others in groups of threes, and some, like the Scotch pine, showing a bare two at each point. Walking in a pine forest assumes an additional interest when every cone underfoot tells a story of the tree from which it fell, and emphasises the wonder of a Nature which can infallibly attach this discriminating sense, as one might almost call it, to every monarch of the forest, compelling the parent to commit unerringly to its progeny, not merely its general form and semblance, its habit and habitat, but its every essential curve and characteristic, even to the points at which its pip-curves shall intersect, so that, without outside interference, no white pine had ever the spirals of the yellow, nor bore the same number of needles as the Scotch nor bent the same curves as the Oregon;—ah, surely these things give one pause.

The actual formation of the Pinus strobus will be, it seems, of sufficient interest to warrant the reproduction of the diagram, in

[1] Appendix, Note XXIV.

which, it need hardly be said, that only the four chief radii vectors
are shown, the remainder being left to the imagination, being, indeed,

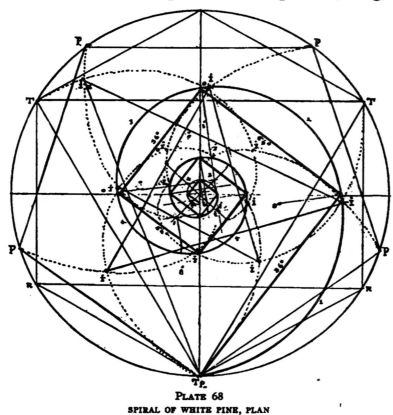

PLATE 68
SPIRAL OF WHITE PINE, PLAN

infinite. The form of the pip-curves comes plainly into view in the
dotted lines of the spiral of three by five, as illustrated in plate 68
the correlating description of which may be put thus:

Pinus strobus, being of the three plus five order, renders the general plan with spirals of the one plus one and one plus two classes, and in this case a given circle must be divided by three and five equal parts, the triangle of 60° appearing on the former and the pentagon on the latter. The spiral of one plus one and one plus two now pinned (as before described) to the centre of the plan and its arcs drawn, the long one on the division by three, and the short one on those by five, the intersections of the spirals will render the proportions of the seed-vessels as they continue towards the centre, the ideal angle passing from the intersecting points of these throughout their diminishing spaces, as at the points I. A secondary spiral, with constant quadrant chords which from the vertical position appear as 36°/54° of the pentagon produced from the pole TP, will pass from point to point of the quadrant vectors of the primary circle, while the similar quadrant arcs of 36°/54° will continue through the intersections of the spirals one plus one and one plus two.

This, in turn, gives us an excellent basis for the study of such things as the upper and lower sides of many beautiful shells, and in plates 69 and 70 we have set out both these sides of the Trochus maximus, to be supplemented in plate 71 by the delicate lines of the spiral of the common snail, over against which, in plate 72 has been placed the cone of the Oregon pine to emphasise the unity of Nature's processes, whether she works at the top of the

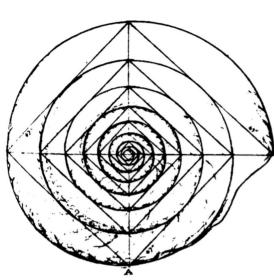

PLATE 69

TROCHUS MAXIMUS

LOOKING DOWN FROM THE APEX

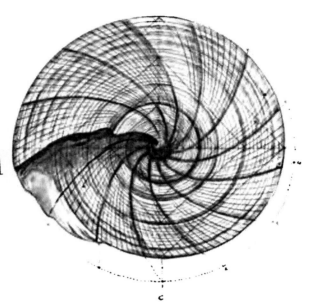

PLATE 70

TROCHUS MAXIMUS

UNDER SIDE OF SPIRAL

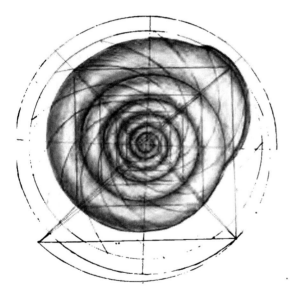

PLATE 71

COMMON SNAIL

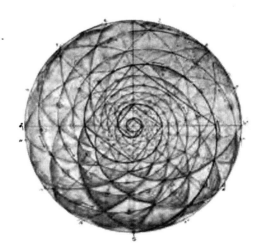

PLATE 72

OREGON PINE CONE

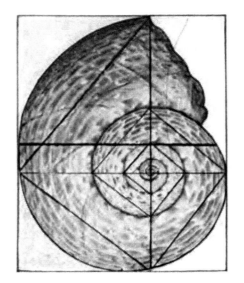

PLATE 73

DOLIUM

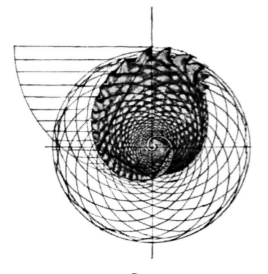

PLATE 74

HALIOTIS CORRUGATA

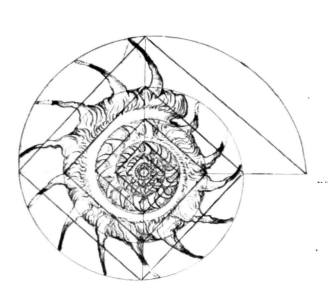

PLATE 75

XENOPHORA SOLARIS

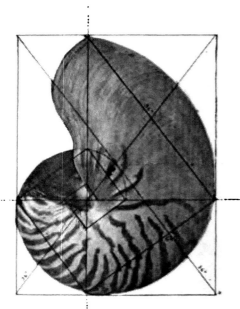

PLATE 76

NAUTILUS

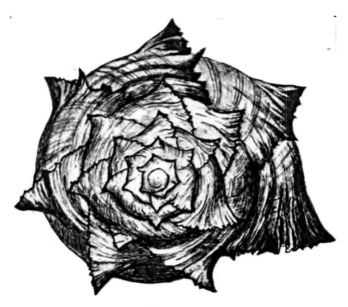

PLATE 77
MUREX

PLATE 78
SCALARIA PRETIOSA

loftiest of trees, or in the damp earth under foot, or in the deeps of the sea.

It is impracticable to give here anything like a completed list of the beautiful shells which one could examine by the process described. A few, however, will be given, and if more be desired, reference must be had to such works as the previous one and many contemporaneous publications[1] and to museums where examples will be found in profusion. In plates 73 to 78 will be found a series of shells, beautiful alike for their markings and their contours. To say that in botany and conchology the spiral idea must be kept constantly in mind would be trite, and in the realm of shells alone is material for a lifetime of study, toward which we can turn but a few brief moments.

Most of the shells shown in the next few illustrations will, with the aid of the diagrams which have preceded them, sufficiently explain themselves. Dolium, our charming friend in plate 73, affords an example of nearly perfect logarithmic spiral with Nautilus, plate 76, a close second, the angles of both being coherent to the family of the golden series. Nautilus, investigated in its inward depths, develops a surprising approximate to the mechanical arrangements of the present turbine, while the shell of the common snail stands at the other limit of construction from Nautilus, the former being exceedingly slim in its spiral curvature, while the latter develops

[1] Appendix, Note XXV.

its motive of expansion with remarkable activity. Xenophora solaris, shown in plate 75, is scarcely more roomy as an apartment than the shell of the snail, and suggests, with its outward projections, a water wheel of the old-fashioned over-shot type, and is measured by a spiral in the ratio of eight to thirteen.

Haliotis corrugata, plate 74, is shown with its plan repeated within a circle by applying the suggestion of Canon Moseley, that, by cutting out the spiral of these shells on a piece of card and pinning it at the focus and revolving it around a circle, both obversely and reversely, marking the spirals as shown on the diagram, the whole plan could be indicated throughout the entire area of the circle.

The plates 77 and 78 showing respectively the delightful spirals of Murex and Scalaria pretiosa scarcely need explanation, which would perhaps but detract from the careful examination to which they are entitled.

In order to leave no reasonable means of understanding the matter which is to confront us untried, let us look into the points suggested by Plate 79. So far, we have undertaken the examination of all spirals as though they were flat and represented only a single plane. In fact, as we have recognised, few of them are perfectly even in surface, nearly all being found either to rise somewhat at the centre or else to consist of a conic surface, as shown in figure A of plate 79 or, still further, to wind around a cylinder as a vine hugs to a post, in a manner forming a spiral helix, as we see it in figure B. The cylinder itself, however, may have a waved surface, entirely aside from the local curves of the spiral, and as the spiral winds around this, its curves become eccentric, being not all centred on the same focus, as we see them in figure C. With these things in mind we are in position

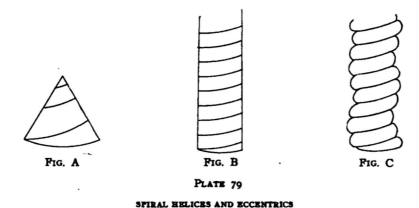

Fig. A   Fig. B   Fig. C

PLATE 79

SPIRAL HELICES AND ECCENTRICS

to take up more intelligently the examination of such examples as the side view of a pine cone, fresh from the forest, or a head of yellow clover as we find it in plate 80, where its spiral formation may be examined without effort. The same general conformation is shown in a side view of Trochus maximus in plate 81 where the radial intervals are shown by transfer at the upper horizontal and a similar method is adopted to develop the details of the upright view of Facelaria in plate 82 where, in addition, the spiral itself is shown in plan

11

at the foot of the shell. That this form of growth is not confined to any one branch of natural reproduction may be seen in plate 83 where sprigs of asparagus are illustrated, with their spirals clearly showing that the tops, at the edible stage, conform to the same set of rules as the pine cone and the clover, in all of which the spirals are double, indicating the nearly orthogonal intersections of the spiral lines as explained by Dr. Church, while in the shell formations the spirals are generally single in form, and consequently asymmetric.

In nearly every grove of fine trees, we shall time after time find ourselves admiring great boles which have become twisted and curved in the course of their maturity into all sorts of helical spirals, sometimes the markings run around the bark like a clinging vine, and sometimes they curve with the knots of the wood. Looking at plate 84 we have a case in point, and numberless others await us at every shady nook, which need hardly be sketched here; but amongst them may always be found many perfect single spirals. Most of us in this world of imperfections are quite elated when we find ourselves competent to do any one thing correctly, as these spiral-twisted trees have done, and this rule is largely followed in botany as well as in conchology, but not by beautiful begonia. Begonia is like a coy child who curls a wisp of hair into a spiral helix around her finger, and then, embarrassed, twists it the other way. Only, begonia elects to do both of these things at once, and in plate 85 we see her forming one of the

PLATE 80

YELLOW CLOVER

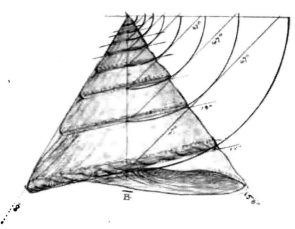

PLATE 81

TROCHUS MAXIMUS

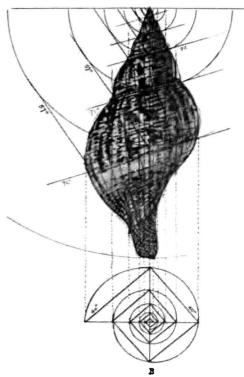

B

PLATE 82

FACELARIA

PLATE 83

ASPARAGUS

comparatively few examples of both a right-hand and left-hand spiral, separately and yet completed in the same element of growth, finished and visible to the eye. When a helianthus or a pine cone forms spirals of two kinds, they are woven in common, cross over, intersect, confuse,

PLATE 84

ELBOW OF MONTEREY CYPRESS

PLATE 85

BEGONIA

and generally complicate each other. When begonia grows two spirals she places each of them just as cosily together as they can possibly be and not quarrel, but they are definite and distinct entities to the end, such as we seldom see in one formation.

With this beautiful example of spirals in both directions before us, it is hardly possible to refrain from a few words on the subject of this distinction. There have been any number of ways of designating these two so that they might be recognised, and all authors do not agree on accepting the same phrases as distinguishing the one from the other. In this, despite our expressed desire to avoid unnecessary technicalities in this work, we find ourselves in the position of taking refuge in the scientific terminology, which, once understood, is of course more determinative in the end than homely terms. Familiar expressions, just because they are familiar, are apt to be read with a prejudged and not always correct meaning. The names right-hand and left-hand, as applied to spirals, sound very easy but they prove as misleading in application in conchology as frequently they do in a military description. In heraldry, I need hardly say, that the right or dexter side of the shield is the side which is to the right of the bearer when the shield is on his arm, and hence, is the left-hand side to the spectator. This much is simple, but what is meant by "the right of the line," for instance, depends on the context. If we refer to our own line, it means, of course our own right, facing, as soldiers should, toward the enemy. If, on the contrary, we refer to the enemy's line, then we mean *his* right, which as we face it is our left, so that in charging the enemy's right it is one's own left which is brought into action.

A conchologist will designate his shells by the side upon which the opening faces, and, in a univalve, if a shell stands in front of him and the apex is placed up, he will say that it is a right-hand spiral if the aperture faces him from the right side and, conversely, that it is a left-hand or sinistral shell if it opens from the left side. Looking at the two examples which are shown in plates 86 and 87 we find that, by this test, the one in plate 86 is a right-hand or dextral and the other a left-hand or sinistral shell. Yet nearly any one examining these offhand would certainly have the feeling that the names did not accord with his impression, and that, to him, the names should be reversed and it is curious to note that in several classes, shells of both kinds may be found in one genus, as with the Red Whelk, in which the læotropic form prevails amongst the living examples and the dexiotropic amongst the fossils.

To avoid all of this, we find that the conchologists have added yet another term to their already weighty list, or perhaps I should say a pair of terms: and these, new perhaps though they be to some readers, nevertheless have the merit of being determinative, as I have said, and may easily be remembered when their meanings are understood. It has been ingenuously said that "if an insect, walking in at the opening of such a shell (plate 86) proposes to reach the central point, that insect will have to keep on turning to the left until it reaches its destination, that being the reason why such a shell is called læotropic [turning to the left]." Equally, and because it is a shell formed according to the spiral shown in plate 87, the same insect, or another equally inquisitive, if the first had grown dizzy with the left-hand turnings, would have to wind continually to the right to reach the focus, and so this would be called dexiotropic.

PLATE 86

FUSUS—A LÆOTROPIC SPIRAL
From *Nature's Harmonic Unity*

PLATE 87

CHRYSODOMUS ANTIQUUS
A Dexiotropic Spiral

The dexiotropic spiral, it will be noted, follows the sun as the hands of the clock do in their motions, and is sometimes called "clock-wise," while the læotropic form disputes the sun and, if little Alice could come back from Wonderland, she would doubtless call it "un-clockwise" We shall, however, leave these things largely to the scientists, together with the extremely interesting questions of whether a wearer of horns comes within the homonymous or heteronymous class, which, being interpreted means, whether he parts his horns in the middle and curls his right-hand horn in a right-hand spiral, and his left one conversely, or whether he wears his right horn twisted to the left and vice versa.

It would also be of great interest to search out botanically those forms of climbing plants which "follow the sun" in a dexiotropic spiral and those which go against it læotropically. It is enough to state that large numbers do one and many do the other, and the botanists shall if they can tell us why. As an enthusiastic gardener I can say without fear of contradiction, that sundry legumes and considerable garden truck, unlike the hop vine, coil around the pole in the direction opposite the path of the sun, while many vines and grapes are dexiotropic. We may be certain, however, that whatever purpose Nature has in the distribution of her spiral choice, man has always had more or less superstition on the subject and very early began to count the spiral or whorl which followed the sun as an omen of good, and the counter-spiral as a portent of evil, and a number of the old legends and customs relating to this singular question have been gathered together by Sir Theodore Cook in his *Curves of Life* in one of which tradition tells us that at the baptism of a Lithuanian infant, the parents bury one of its little curls at the foot of a hop pole so that the child "may twine out of danger" in its life time, just as the hop vine twines upward toward the sun.

We find also many of the symbolic columns of ancient architecture decorated with these sun-following spirals. This is true of the four columns behind the high altar of San Marco at Venice, which legend says were taken from the temple of Solomon at Jerusalem. Such a series of references to benevolent emblems and their converse, can hardly be permitted to stop short of the mention of the Svastika, that four-legged figure intended perhaps for a conventionalised form of spiral, and common as a decoration nearly the world over from the time of the ancients. It is thought to bring good fortune to those who hold objects in which its decoration runs sun-wise and the worst of ill-luck when it runs the other way.[1]

It is necessary, however, to take all of these things with a grain of salt, not merely as to our belief in the potency of the charm but in the weight we credit the superstition as having even with those who held it. Perhaps as an assurance to the incredulous and half-credulous, Christianity itself in its early stages conformed so frequently to the popular beliefs in these particulars as that the early designs in decoration used in the churches seldom were allowed to embody in any superstitious form a symbol which would be hateful to the pagans. Yet I recollect too many beautiful læotropic columns of great antiquity now serving conspicuously in noble churches where they have stood from early times, to give the circumstance too great weight. Take, for example, the exquisite pillars in exquisite variety

[1] Further descriptive reference to the Svastika will be made later. Also App., Note XXXI.

which surround the charming *chiostro* of the church of San Paolo fuori le Mura, where twisted column follows twisted column, spiral succeeds spiral, some right, some left, some with both entwined together,

PLATE 88

SAN PAOLO FUORI LE MURA

some plain helices and some as eccentric as Bacchus, and all with a beauty far beyond the poor pencil with which I have sketched them in plate 88.

Where every uncurling of a fern presents spiral forms worthy of a Bishop's crozier and every twisting vine in sight suggests the pattern of a beautiful column, the subjects are well-nigh endless, and with one exception those that remain must take their place in a succeeding chapter among the mere works of man himself; but the present subject can hardly close without one longing look at a few of the most beautiful of all those spiral things which are the work of Nature, unassisted by the hand or brain of the lords of creation. To every huntsman, whether he enter the chase with powder or camera, the head-dress of the "beautifully antlered deer and the goat so lightly springing" are the rewards of no mean order. So here hang our trophies. Four pair of natural spirals for man to emulate in his works: The Greek Moufflon in plate 89, stocky and "crooked as a ram's horn" should proverbially be offset by the curving grace of the dignified pair of calipers which the self-possessed Axis (plate 90) wears with so Chesterfieldian an air. These are worthy foil to the heteronymous ornaments of the Wallachian sheep in plate 91 and the marvellously constructed horns of the African Koodoo in plate 92, where he is shown at perhaps his very best, which is very good indeed.

One would like to go on indefinitely, but time and space forbid,[1] and the frequency of the introduction of the spiral into art and architecture has been so marked as to require attention as a subject

[1] See many other beautiful forms of this kind mentioned in Appendix, Note XXV.

PLATE 89
GREEK MOUFFLON
From Nature

PLATE 90
AXIS MACULATA
From Nature

PLATE 91
WALLACHIAN SHEEP

PLATE 92
KOODOO
Hooker

by itself. With this in mind I have endeavoured to confine the examples in this chapter to those arising outside these realms, reserving them in turn for later consideration.

ASYMMETRICAL GROUPS

It will have been kept in mind that each of these non-circular curves may be created on any of the basic groupings which were brought out earlier. A catenary may be depicted on the angle of 30° and its complement of 60° and develop all the elementary ideas of the family to which that species belongs, or it may be created on any other combination, and only the case in point at the moment can be given consideration in this regard. The same is true of ellipses and ovals, eccentrics and spirals, but in spite of the mathematical indifference, if I might so denominate it, Nature seems to have certain preference for definite forms to perform given service, as in choosing the ellipse for orbital revolutions of the planets in preference to a spiral motion such as she indicates in nebulæ. This may be seen reflected in the fact that she advances many more catenary curves which are related directly to the tetragon group than to other modules, due, perhaps to the fact that polar force is influential in so many directions which generally develop these lines. Again, as we could see in the examination of shells and many examples of flowers and the

study of phyllotaxis, the spirals which she produces are largely logarithmic and based with great frequency on the golden series of extreme
and mean ratio. All of these things develop from the examination of
the instances cited in the pages which we have gone over, and all are
in strict keeping with the tendencies in natural force, expansion, and
reproduction which have from time to time been taken up. The
spirals of the various pine cones, for instance, are fit examples of the
life principal on the serial lines of extreme and mean proportion.[1] The
ratios in integers, counting each pip as wholly developed and completed at any one moment, are, as we have seen, 3:5, 5:8, and 8:13.
Considered from the non-fractional point of view and as an ever continuing growth in which each spiral stands revealed as an uncompleted,
expanding, vibrant thing, we at once recognise the golden series as
the ready and accurate module, just as has been so often expressed
before in these pages and in our previous work on this subject.

Of all curves it is easy to accept the spiral as being the most
beautiful. What it loses from homogeneity as compared with the
circle, it gains in the sense of freedom and expansion. It might indeed
be the true symbol of growth, slipping smoothly ever onward and
upward, a route inviting the very soul to the eternal spaces.

[1] Appendix, Note XXXIII.

CHAPTER VI

THE GOLDEN SERIES IN NATURE

WERE we to depend for our study of Nature upon the evidence produced under the examination of inorganic forms and the laws governing gravity and the other forces which control movement, we should inevitably come to the conclusion that she recognised practically nothing but tetragonal relations. If, on the other hand, we examine the animal and vegetable kingdoms, we shall find them teeming with illustrations of pentagonal form and shall be faced with instances of continuous extreme and mean proportion from the early rising of the sun even unto the going down of the same. If all of force might properly be symbolised by the square and the hexagon, then, as we have seen, the vital principle of growth might almost take as its type the golden series which is the outgrowth of the Divine section of Euclid, along with the pentagram which in so marvellous a manner develops at every angle and on every side that indefinitely continuous extreme and mean ratio which enters so largely into all productive species.

Great emphasis was laid in our preceding work on the importance of the principle of this continuous series both in natural development and in art and design and in architecture, and the infinite pertinacity with which this module came into play and could be utilised constructively, while a large number of the drawings of that work show by direct and explicit line and intersection the point where this influence concentrates or is disclosed. All this is not enough, nor is it enough that the emphasis should lie between covers other than these; and so again let me say that the golden series or this continuous form of extreme and mean ratio "is one of the greatest factors for the just development of proportional spaces in flowers, plants, shells, and other natural objects, and that upon this series a theory may be advanced that will supply a substantial proportion of the requirements of all students in the art of design." Let me repeat also that in this form "extreme and mean proportion is one of the most vital among all modules employed by Nature, and is easily recognised throughout all forms of growth"; and again say, that "too much importance can hardly be attributed in a work of this kind to the principle of extreme and mean ratio, for there are few objects in living forms of Nature which do not reveal its effect, thus declaring the law to be one of the fundamentals of true proportion."[1]

[1] Appendix, Note XXVI.

In the introductory explanations, some stress was laid upon the exact perfection with which the pentagram typified the golden series and this was again referred to elsewhere. Let us put this to the test and learn if it works out in real plant-life by comparing such a blossom as the aquilegia or columbine with the web with which we have grown familiar. In plate 93 we have an opportunity to compare actuality in the aquilegia with theory as developed in plate 9 and to see how the columbine tucks itself into every line and corner of this figure and emphasises, if emphasis were needed, the statements before made and the truth with which they were propounded.

We have before referred to the recognised fact, or call it romance, superstition, tradition, what you will, concerning the luck symbol known as the svastika, and presently we shall have more to say on that subject, but one can hardly pass the pentacle without referring to the somewhat similar tradition of long standing in regard to its influence on health and the general welfare of mankind. Of this pentacle or pentagram, Forman says in the *Journal* of the British Archæological Association that probably it was the figure which we know as the five-pointed star so carefully studied by Pythagoras and his followers. It is the same pentagram to which we have referred in the description of the pentagon, and from time immemorial has been the companion of witchcraft and magic. It is not difficult to remember how, being unexpectedly—and unwillingly—visited by the King, Hugh de Yester, Lord Gifford though he was,

> Tarried not his garb to change,
> But, in his wizard habit strange
> Came forth,—a quaint and fearful sight;
> His mantle lined with fox-skins white;
> His high and wrinkled forehead bore
> A pointed cap, such as of yore
> Clerks say that Pharaoh's Magi wore;
> His shoes were mark'd with cross and spell,
> Upon his breast a pentacle.

Here, however, as in the case of sun-twisting spirals, I am lead to doubt Lord Gifford's own faith in his spells, pentacles, and magic, for you will recollect that in spite of all this array of wonder-producing properties, he seems to have felt that he yet lacked somewhat of absolute security, since it appears that, even in his own Bo-Hall and in the face of all this supernatural assistance, nevertheless, when he so hurriedly came forth,

> In his hand he held prepared,
> A naked sword without a guard,

Many observers, who have concluded apparently that only the six-pointed star could be created from the trigon, have by this been led into calling the hexagonal outline a pentagram—an evident misnomer.

In the sphere of absolutely inorganic life we have already noted
a great preponderance of examples formed on the relations of the
square, and amongst these therefore we shall find practically no
examples of pentagonal form and hence must leave those classes

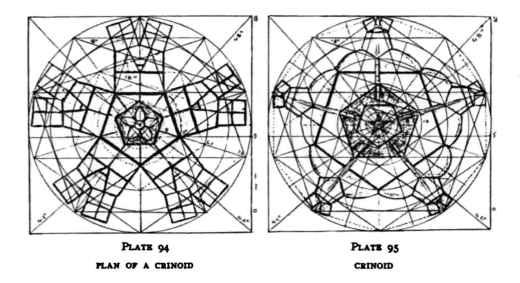

PLATE 94

PLAN OF A CRINOID

PLATE 95

CRINOID

out in our perusal of the five-pointed family and go directly to the
innumerable and fascinating asteroids and crinoids and echinoderms
where we shall net a number of interesting specimens to add to our
collection. What, for instance, could more perfectly illustrate the
point in question than the two plates 94 and 95, showing the "ground
plan" of two of these crinoids.

12

In plate 94 one notes with pleasure that the perimeter of the figure forms the perfect pentagon, but how is this interest increased upon observing that the first progression of the pentagon is distinctly marked on the arms, while the second progression of the same figure exactly coincides with the arm juncture and forms in turn the central structure upon which is built the pentagram, as shown in plates 8 and 9 in the second chapter. Examining now plate 95 we find that, while in the infinite variety which is Nature's chiefest charm, these details do not occur in the same order, yet there they are, specifically delineating the points of interest and drawing as with ruler and compass the progressing pentagons, alternating them, one with its apex upwards, and the next with the base at the top and each ending in the centre with a perfect star.

These examples are, however, only a beginning of the wonders which Nature has wrought along this line, for we have but to turn to plates 96 and 97 to see the same lines almost duplicated in other forms of life, lowly it is true, but nevertheless demonstrating, beyond quibble, this power of Nature to select what best suits her. Plate 96 shows us the outlined form of an antedon, which might be a mere geometrical diagram for all the observable deviation from mathematical perfection. In this case, it could properly be descriptively correlated as a perimeter which forms the lines of a pentagon circumscribed about a circle, while the interior forms the second progression of the same beautiful figure and supports, in turn, a star, from which depends other pentagons and pentagrams with microscopic exactness.

The other is an echinoderm shown in plate 97, which might have been selected by the first astronomer for his illustration of one of the

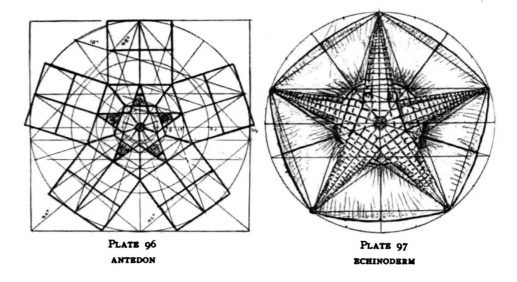

PLATE 96
ANTEDON

PLATE 97
ECHINODERM

heavenly symbols, so definite is it, but, in turn, no more adapted than any other of its kind to the purpose before us all of these being axiomatic in their demonstration and so clear that no more easily read proof is possible to conceive.

Since this is not a work on biology, I may be pardoned if I attempt no differentiation between the many classes of these echinodermata. The Sea-Urchin family is a very large and complicated one, the study of which would repay a scientist, but in which we should be at once lost in the maze of distinctions beyond our immediate purpose. It will be amply sufficient if I say in brief that these asteroids, the crinoids, and the antedons are all members of the family of the echinoderms, and, in support of their pentagonal tendencies, I quote no less an authority than Doctor Bather, curator of Geology in the British Museum who says of them, that "they live in salt or brackish water, and show radial symmetry (sometimes incomplete) of which five is usually the dominant number."[1]

Before leaving the briny quarters of these inhabitants of the deep who are so properly called the echinoderms or "prickly-skinned ones," let us indulge ourselves by taking a look at the developed form of a starfish as shown in plate 98, and then spend a moment over the charms of plate 99 in which we see the full pattern of one of the asteroidæ with literally "line upon line and line upon line," but observe how consistently these details of the pattern carry out our original five-pointed pentagram in their every angle and curve, finishing, so far as developed, with a wonderful star in the centre, of which a correlating description will bring out the fact that this beautifully decorated object is developed from the pentagon as are all of the others. That figure appears to characterise these creations, while the hexagon estab-

[1] Francis Arthur Bather, M.A., D.Sc., F.R.S., F.R.G.S., *Echinoderms.*

PLATE 93

AQUILEGIA

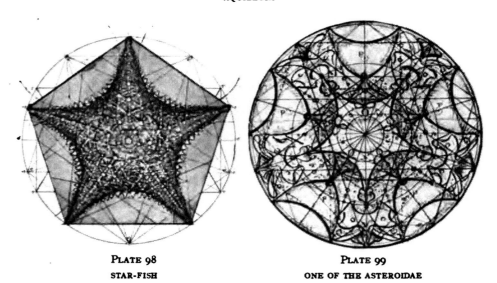

PLATE 98

STAR-FISH

PLATE 99

ONE OF THE ASTEROIDAE

lishes the proportion of the majority of diatoms, although the pentagon
sometimes, but more rarely, has the primary influence. All of these
examples have the rectangle of five plus eight in evidence in various
places of their proportional spaces, as well as the ideal angle. Four
progressions of the pentagon render the chief proportional spaces of
the diagram and a pentagon escribed on the outer arc of this figure
will develop the outer circle on which five smaller circles of the same
dimension as that of the second progression will produce the five arcs
on the rim; and if the same circle is placed with its centre on the
point *d* it will approximate the curve on the central five-pointed star,
though probably this is in fact a catenary curve. The circle of the
first progression of the pentagon taken upon the compasses will then,
with the points where the small interior circles intersect the outer
pentagon as centres, describe the arcs passing through the black dots
at the extremities of the dark five-pointed star. This is one of the
most remarkable examples I know of the correlation of progressing
circles and is well worthy of study.

So much for these lower orders in our biological progress. Then
we feel entitled to take up a higher order, and the beauties of botany
attract us immediately. To show how perfectly these apply to the
form we are studying, a glance at the plan of a wood-sorrel will repay
us, as laid out in plate 100 below, of which extended explanation is
quite unnecessary.

This outline of wood-sorrel, familiar to every lover of outdoors, gives us a taste of what to expect in the way of botany, and is so diagrammatic in its completeness that one only needs to compare it with the illustrations of the pentagram and the golden series earlier

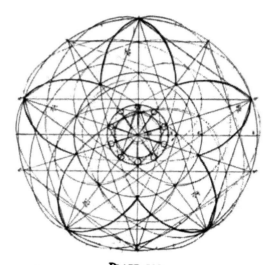

PLATE 100
PLAN OF WOOD-SORREL

in the work to feel the significance; and in describing the correlations of the example we should find that this flower, having five petals, declares at once that the pentagon will interpret its proportional parts, while its curves must be those produced by one of the angles of this figure. If, therefore, the ellipse forming the edge of any petal be continued (as shown by the dotted lines), it will be found that the

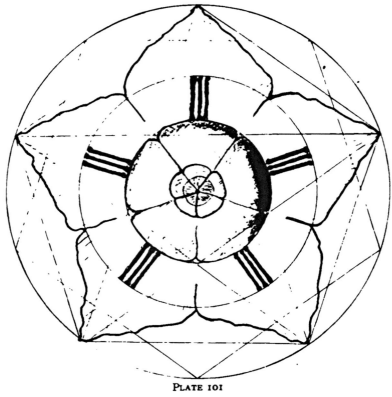

PLATE 101

PYROLA

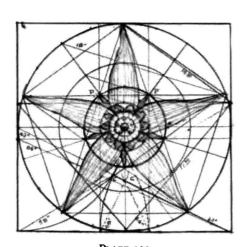

PLATE 102

LOOSESTRIFE

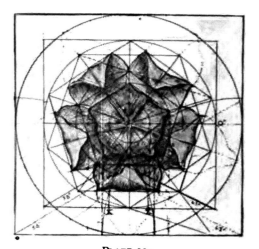

PLATE 103

PITCHER PLANT

transverse axis of the completed ellipse coincides with the angle of 72° of the pentagon, and the same curve will be found to pass directly through each of the five petals, taken in succession. It will be noted that the ellipses intersect on the circle marked 5, which is that inscribed in the pentagon of the first progression, while similar smaller circles enclose the torus with its system of stamens and pistils, all maintaining the correlations of the pentagon.

Further it will be seen that this *oxalis* exemplifies, as do most pentamerous forms, both the golden series and also extreme and mean proportion in its integral correlative.

To illustrate exactly what I mean, I might quote the botanist, Gray, who thus describes the flower of wood-sorrel: "Sepals five, pistils five, bases somewhat united, stamens ten, usually membranous, five-celled and more or less five-lobed."

Then take up plate 101, Pyrola, and make a passing comparison between the correlations seen on the one, those evidenced by the other, and the diagrams in the chapter on family relations, which was perhaps grudgingly read at first but which will now be seen to have very definite meaning and will show, as in plates 8 and 9 all the symmetry of the pentagonal form of extreme and mean proportion.

Looking again at plate 93, and reminding ourselves of how exactly our columbine fitted into the sharp angles of the pentagram, turn now to plate 102 and compare columbine with loosestrife.

Make a similar comparison between the outlines of the pitcher plant
in plate 103 and the starfish in plate 98 and the crinoids in plates 94
and 95. See how, in the pitcher plant, the umbrella-shaped top of the
pistil is the exact form of the pentagon in the second progression, with
five petals overarching it, and all in a constant extreme and mean
proportion.   And the continuity of these pentagonal examples can
scarcely fail while such instances remain as the skyward and earth-
ward sides of Parnassia to be added in plates 104 and 105. Each of
these will be found to be perfectly pentagonal, but each displays
features entirely distinct, yet pressing continually the lesson, and
nearly every one furnishes at least a pair of ratio-filled stars. This is
perhaps particularly noticeable in plate 105 where Parnassia furnishes
us three distinct sets. The five petals of the corolla form the inner
(and in this case, lower) circle, followed by the five sepals of the calyx,
which give us a second pentagram, and topping these we have the
cup clasping all together in a perfect pentagon. And it should be
noted further that each set of these configurations bears not only the
stamp of extreme and mean proportion in itself, but that in its size to
its next larger unit, the golden progression is also perfect. Thus the
petals are enclosed in the prime circle, the sepals in the second progression and the inner pentagon of the cup by the fourth, indicating
a perfect relation of the golden series between all of these parts. This
is true not alone of Parnassia, but may be interestingly followed out

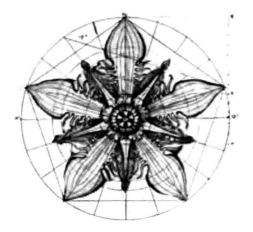

PLATE 104
PARNASSIA

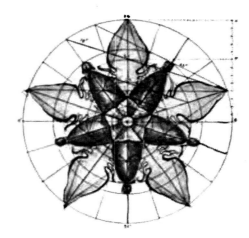

PLATE 105
PARNASSIA

PLATE 106
HENBANE

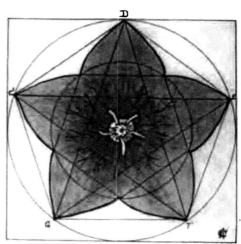

PLATE 107·
JAPANESE BELL FLOWER

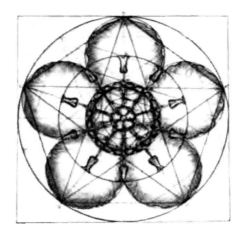

PLATE 108

PIPSISSEWA

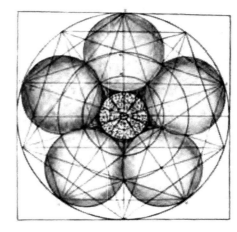

PLATE 109

SPIREA VAN HOUTI

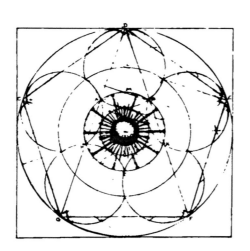

PLATE 110

WILD ROSE

PLATE III

WOODBINE

with each of the others as shown in the diagrams, 106, Henbane, and 107, Platycodon (Japanese Bellflower).

Further examples are perhaps scarcely needed to show the pertinacity with which Nature calls upon the five-pointed form in her botanical system, but their introduction will at least serve to amplify this frequency and to emphasise the fact that if, as several writers are bold to state, she has no intention nor meaning in this selection, she has at least found it secretly profitable, and if the choice has been "accidental" the accident has been so far successful that, after generations of plant life, she has seen no reason for discarding the results of the choice. We are learning every day that Nature never does anything without a purpose. If vegetation is green, it is now conceded that it is because in her infinite knowledge (or shall we call it her infinitely perfected gambling system) she finds that the actinic properties absorbed through the screen of a green surface, are conducive to plant growth. Hence, as plants die out and no longer have use for this productive aid, they invariably lose their green as they lose their sap, and life dies out. If then, this be chance, how fortunate that chance, and why does it so seldom vary?

At the venture, therefore, four plates are added, appropriate to this subject: plate 108, the Pipsissewa, plate 109, the Spirea Van Houti, plate 110, the Wild Rose, and plate 111, a Leaf of the Woodbine.

In the successive order of importance, having seen that Nature seldom shows herself as governing inorganic matter, nor mere force, by other than members of what we have called the tetragon family and that in the lower ranks of biology she, on the other hand, evidences a constant trend toward the influence of the golden series and shows this both directly in measurements and by the constant use of the pentagon and pentagram, which are the very prototypes of continuous extreme and mean proportion, it is now logical to examine farther into the subject by seeking illustrations from the animal kingdom, and at last from mankind, as the superior of them all.

Few of us will have far to go in search of a faithful dog, either our own or another's, and even from this lowly friend one may without much trouble obtain evidence of the tendency to which I have referred. No dog lover will need much instruction on the subject, for most of us will have seen outlines in many forbidden places which look strikingly like the diagrammatic sketch of wood-sorrel but which were, in fact, Bertillon records of the whereabouts or the has-been-abouts of some canine pet. Compare, now, plate 112 which shows the foot of an adult hound with any of the previous illustrations, especially plate 100, and let the facts come home to us.

Then, since man, after all, is more interested in himself than in any other animal, let us spend a period in introspection, for which purpose, I would have you turn to plates 113, 114, and 115 in which are shown the hand, the arm, and the leg of the composite human.

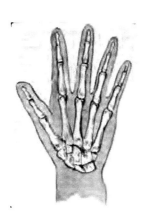

PLATE 113
ANATOMY OF THE HUMAN
HAND

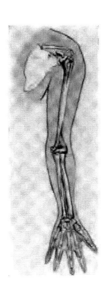

PLATE 114
BONES OF THE HAND
AND ARM

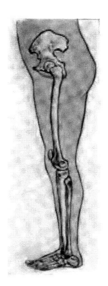

PLATE 115
BONES OF THE LEG
AND FOOT

Taking up, first, plate 113, showing a composite drawing from X-ray views of the hand, we find it so full of exemplifications of the golden series as almost to defy the preparation of a complete list, and of these it is unnecessary to mention more than the obvious one that the bones, from the ungual phalanges to their respective metacarpals, are in a proportion of length and width nicely adjusted by this series of which

PLATE 112
FOOT OF A HOUND

we speak. In the same way, the distances between the wrist and elbow, the elbow and the collar bone are related, and this holds good also as between the foot, the knee, and the hip. Again "the widest part of the thigh bears this relation to the narrowest part, the width of the leg at the calf, with the ankle, the forearm with the wrist, the thumb with the middle finger, and so on indefinitely."[1]

It is well known that the Greeks, studying the human figure

Nature's Harmonic Unity, page 182.

constantly, and choosing it as the subject of those monuments of the plastic art which have come down to us as the best of all classic standards, set for themselves, and thus for all generations to come, a canon

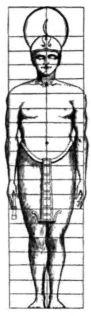

Plate 116

EGYPTIAN CANON
AS ACCEPTED BY
POLYCLITUS

of measurement which was the module followed from their day to our own. In this we constantly commemorate the celebrated Doryphorus of Polyclitus, in which the forefinger was used as the module, nineteen times this being the height of the figure, as shown in plate 116, which represents the still older Egyptian canon from which Polyclitus is thought to have taken his standard.

The Greeks however, quickly realising that varying subjects required varying treatment, gradually divided their subjects into three classes, the tall and slender, with a height of eight heads, the medium, with a height of seven and a half heads, and the short and muscular, with a height of seven heads; the first of these, rendering a total height eight times the measurement of the head, being the customary basis.

For the purpose of illustrating the relation borne by such a figure to the extreme and mean proportion which is so closely allied with the pentagon in all forms, an examination of plate 117 will well repay

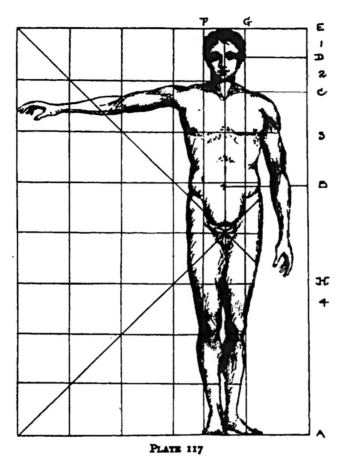

PLATE 117

RELATION OF THE GREEK CANON TO A SERIES IN EXTREME AND MEAN PROPORTION
From *Nature's Harmonic Unity*

The squares at the left show the Greek Canon as in plate 166 of the former work, and the divisions on the right express the relations in terms of the Golden Series as set out in pages 181 *et seq.* (*idem.*), and in the text.

189

the time spent. This figure is reproduced here from the pages of *Nature's Harmonic Unity* and the interesting marginal comments are those taken from the text of that work from which it will be noted that the total height is accurately divided at the umbilical point into extreme and mean proportion, falling at the line marked (B) on the diagram. The balance of the height, constituting as it does the lesser of the two terms of the extreme and mean ratio, is then again divided into the same proportion at C, the division falling at the neck, and this, repeated, brings a further division at the eyes. Quoting from the former work it may be further said that "it will be seen also that an extreme and mean ratio exists as between the height and width of the shoulders, and that the horizontal line marking the division into this ratio will place the umbilicus, in one case, and the length of the arm, in the other. If extreme and mean ratio be again applied, it will be found to measure the relation between the width of the head at the eyes with the width of the throat, while various parts of the body will be found related in the same manner," and as already quoted "the widest part of the thigh bears this relation to the narrowest part, the width of the leg at the calf with the ankle, the forearm with the wrist, and so on indefinitely."[1]

Were any doubt remaining of the prevailing effect of this propor-

[1] *Nature's Harmonic Unity*, by same authors. Putnam, 1912. Plates 166 and 168, pages 181, 183, and 289. And Appendix, Note XXVII post.

tion upon the human body, it might be dispelled by a glance at the figure of a young man with his arms upraised, or the correlations of the Hermes of Praxiteles as shown in the preceding book, to which this is supplementary. In all of these the influence of the golden series and the pentagon is so clear as to be truly predominant.

It is interesting as well to note that since the publication of the book in question others have found time and mind to support theories of this influence and the proportioning effect and powers of this great series upon anatomy. In the same way, in his splendid work *The Curves of Life*, Sir Theodore Cook finds the divisions of the human body proportioned to this series, much as I have quoted them from *Nature's Harmonic Unity* and as we find them illustrated in plate 117. In his example this writer finds that in a well built man, the distance from the ground to the navel represents one stage of this series, the portion from the navel to the crown of the head another, while this latter space, on return, may be found divided at the line of the breasts by another step in keeping with the series: all of which are an interesting and valuable confirmation which Sir Theodore carries out by a figure of an artist's model into which the statements have been incorporated, and which adds to the value of the work.[1] This writer also carries the matter through art and architecture with the aid of a Franz Hals and a Botticelli, both of which serve to maintain the

[1] *Curves of Life*, Sir T. A. Cook, Constable, 1914.

stand as taken, but which, not being part of the evidence furnished by Nature on the subject, are, perhaps, no part of this subdivision of our effort.

We shall have more to say about the golden series, the pentagram, and extreme and mean ratio in the remaining pages, but, in so far as they have to do with Nature rather than the arts and works of man, the more we study her the more fully and firmly are we convinced that what has been said in our former writings had all of the force of minor prophecy. It becomes daily more apparent that, as I had before said "we shall ever find the evidences of this ratio and its operation as a measuring rod, flung broadcast throughout all Nature. From a long study of Nature's employment of this proportion I venture to say that, whenever it appears that Nature is making use of any series, a scientific analysis will almost invariably show that what she aims at is the perfect and indefinitely continuous and accurate extreme and mean proportion." What else, one may ask, shall we expect to find, where testimonials are so unending and so frequently point in the same way? How else should Nature exercise that perfect stability of purpose which we well know is her dominant characteristic, without ever being guilty of a moment's monotony, such as would arise from a constant repetition?

Examination has shown what the power of the tetragon and its relations may become when sought in realms of force, and we have now examined, scantily it is true, but with some care, nevertheless, the pervading influence of the golden series in life. Had we space, we could go with equal interest into the scarcely touched realms of the solid, the pyramidal, the four-dimensional, and other forms in addition to the linear, superficial, and spiral which have been our main study because bringing matters to a focus with least "hewing of wood and drawing of water" which such research necessarily involves. If now, we must turn to such examples as are the work of men's hands and brains, and thus leave the spontaneous proofs afforded by Nature less in the foreground we shall at least see what use man has made of the facts disclosed.

The golden series is indeed a type, as has been emphasised, of life itself, perfect at every step, containing in itself the very germ of continuity, capable of endless extension into the measureless future, returning upon itself and to its beginning never; unlike the circle, extending ever onwards, limited by no radius nor diameter, content to stop or potent to go forward! Small wonder, perhaps, that the ancients, who saw but a portion of it, nevertheless, of that portion, thought it golden and called it divine.

13

CHAPTER VII

PROPORTIONAL FORM AS APPLIED IN ART AND ARCHITECTURE

PATIENT examination of all of these long and perhaps tedious details has brought us to the point where it is possible to make a proper estimate regarding our material. Does it appear from what we have seen that it is probable, nay, certain, that, in her manifold and beautiful development of the Heavens and the Earth and the things under the Earth subject to that Divine hand which guides and controls all, Nature finds it profitable to govern her works very largely by certain forms which we have described,—the tetragon family, the family of extreme and mean proportion, including the pentagon, and various spirals? If it seems to the reader as it does to the writers, that these things have been established beyond peradventure, then we are again brought face to face with the secondary question, whether or not we shall disregard all of the testimony of legend, writ, and patent results as handed down to us, and suppose, contrary to the evidence of all of these, that mankind has builded all of his works "out of his own head" without reference to those things which were constantly going on around him. With what seemed to

194

the writers conclusive proof, both of these questions have been answered specifically.[1]

The purpose, then, of the work now before us, as of the former one, is to see in what manner these regulations, constantly in use by Nature, have been put to use and followed by man. Has he been guided somewhat by the square and the equilateral triangle, as Nature is in her demonstrations of force, and has he utilized the delicate possibilities of the golden series and spiral in his constantly accumulating works? It is not enough for one in the era in which we live to ask whether or no our artists and architects and designers do consciously hark back to Nature at every turn. The human race has existed for æons of ages and the life of a man is but a span long. It therefore follows that, did every man begin his investigations where his father in turn began, no progress would ever be possible. Not long ago a man very successful in making money was so foolish as to remark that he never paid the slightest attention to history, as he was interested only in the future. Now history, may I remark in turn, is the very basis of every possible accomplishment. Were we minded to set aside the merely political and military history of mankind, how, nevertheless should

---

[1] See Appendix, Note XXVIII. It will not, of course, repay to present here a repetition of the statements of the former work in full, but a consecutive arrangement demands that, since the readers of the present volume may not have the former one before them, the conclusions drawn there be at least referred to, and, using only the outline as above stated for the present text, the necessary basic conclusions from the former work are included in the Appendix.

we go forward in manufacture and chemistry and mechanics and art without the facts which the busy investigators of the past have laid bare to us, and which are the history of those branches? Would the manufacturer beckon himself back to the time when men walked because the wheel had not been discovered, when chemistry went no farther than use as a fetish, or to that age when bronze was the only metal used for tools because steel had not been discovered, and when the earth was insistently called flat and the sun supposed to sail majestically around it? The successive steps whereby man rose superior to these conditions are all a part of history, in which we of this year of grace accept, almost without question, the achievement of the days gone by. So it is in art and architecture. Today, we seldom create standards in these things because those before us have spent so much time and talent in establishing basic foundations which we have come to accept because we have looked upon them and found them good. There was a time, however, when man had to figure everything out for himself, a time when, perforce, he turned to the "sermons in the stones, books in the running brooks," because, forsooth, he had no otherwhere to turn for his standards, no other books to read than those which Nature furnished him. These he read with a truthfulness astonishing to us whose powers of observation are perhaps dulled by the fact that no longer is eternal vigilance the price of safety. Whatever the cause, the effect is that in the accruing centuries, man has adapted himself to the conditions and now accepts what his fathers have unearthed, both in the gold of commerce and in that invaluable golden knowledge which is his heritage, and frequently stops neither to seek the origin nor to thank the originator.

In considering all of these points, while it is clear that the ancients laid out temples and carved monuments and wrought metals on lines which indicate that they followed the indices of Nature's mode, it is unnecessary to presuppose that those ancients understood or pretended to understand at all why Nature did these things. In vast degree we do not understand these points ourselves even today. Clearly Pythagoras lacked even the most rudimentary knowledge of why his string, divided at certain points, resounded in a way which he declared, and all the world since have declared, was agreeable to the ear. He knew nothing whatever about the ratios of vibration nor the laws of sound nor gravity. His sense, however, was sufficiently acute to tell him that the tones produced were musical as the singing of the birds in the branches overhead, and being like the chiel whom Burns reminds us is ever amang us takin' notes he put it all down and the result has come to us today along with the knowledge which has accumulated meanwhile.

Thus it is evident that when we look to Greek architecture and Greek sculpture, and the masters of painting and the arts and crafts in general for our models, we are indirectly accepting whatever basic ideas moved them, and it remains to us only to unearth what these may have been. We call these works "classic" and use them for our own modules. What then shall we not gain if we can determine by what means the ancients hit upon these splendid ideals and upon what they based their proportions? We sometimes stand incredulous at the supposition that these men of old times were careful to follow the dictates of Nature and saw in her uses and customs a wealth of material as to colour and form. Why, pray, should they not, *since they had no other?*

It is worthy attention also to speak of the question of mathematical knowledge and its application. It is sometimes pettily assumed that because we have undertaken to study Nature in her mathematical moods, we have staged her with a pair of compasses in the one hand, and a ruler and table of logarithms in the other. Nature, unfortunately for us, has her mathematics first hand and needs no experimental drawing board to work out her problems, doing so on the face of the great worlds at her disposal. I once heard a famous painter say of an unsigned picture to which exception had been taken because it lacked the manual characters of the painter in the south-east corner, that this "was an utterly immaterial and childish objection, since the painter had *signed the picture all over* by his inimitable touch." That the science of mathematics is needed by poor mortal man in order to work out and eke out his twilight knowledge of great

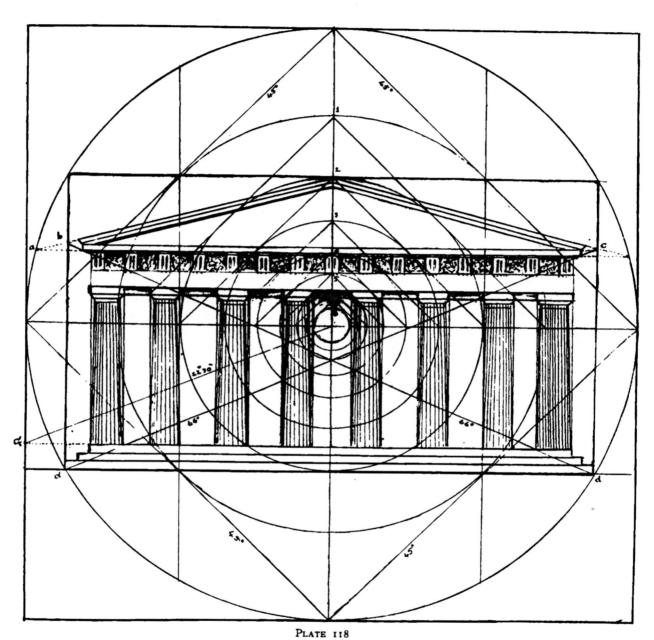

PLATE 118

PARTHENON AND THE SQUARE
(Correlations by Mr. Hambidge)

Nature must not be used as a proof that she, herself, cannot and does not paint her pictures with perfect mathematical precision, as we realise in every examination, and that she cannot and does not do this without the aid of a visible ruler or written rules such as are needed for mankind, for as she paints the picture she records the rules all over it, that he who runs may read, and she signs it on every inch of space, despite the fact that we cannot perhaps see the initials "D. N." on any visible portion of the canvass.

With small doubt that we may find something worth while, then, we turn first, because it is one of the oldest of all the structures to be analysed, to the front portico of the Parthenon, as correlated a number of years ago by Mr. Hambidge from the Penrose measurements, and as shown in *Nature's Harmonic Unity*, and as repeated in plate 118. Criticism of this has been from time to time advanced because Iktinus had frequently indulged in straight lines which were not straight, in order that to the eye the result might appear what, in fact, it actually was, strong and beautiful. To one seriously undertaking such a study as this, a question of the nature indicated seems more or less of a puerile quibble. That the architect should so strenuously desire that his building should appear to the eye exactly what he designed it to be is a compliment to the strength of his own convictions and the strongest possible substantiation of the stand here assumed, to wit, that he was subjugating even the laws of optics in his endeavour to make his building follow, not merely in blind and parrot-like imitation but in the very spirit of Nature's purpose. Has he given his stylobate its gently rising central curve in order to change the mathematical formation or the true perfection? By no means, for this has been done only that the flooring should not only *be* practically and to all intents a perfect plane, but that to the eye viewing it as a whole it should *appear* to be true as well, and not seen to have, as otherwise it would under the laws of optics, a weak and dependent middle section. Has Iktinus given to his columns that gradual swelling outward from the absolute ruled line, in order to change the actual conditions of the structure? Does this "entasis" add to the strength or change the design from the one as it lay on the board before him? No, precisely no. It merely overcomes the optical illusion arising from the position of the observer, who must, from the ground, look upward along a column, with the result that toward the top the lines, if straight, would seem to be curving inwards. For the exact purpose then of making the finished whole appear precisely in result what it was when drawn under the eye, the swelling stylobate and the curving entasis and the slope of the end columns (too slight to be measured in any illustration) were intentionally and cunningly devised. Let me state with all emphasis that these things in no wise change the plan. They artfully enable the builder to convey from the height of the pediment the exact idea the architect wished to convey to the observing eye down on the pavement below, and to make him see in the reality exactly what the architect saw in the drawing.

It would not be necessary to dwell on this explanation were it not that more than once the question has been, perhaps thoughtlessly, asked by those who knew of these artificial means adopted to produce the effects desired, but who did not, it would seem, carry their thought to its logical conclusion.

Let us remember, in this regard and in every study of natural subjects, that "compensation" is the universal condition. No undertaking can be carried out under a single influence, and should we insist that no examples were to be accepted other than those showing the influence of only *one* condition or force, we should end by discarding everything in life. We cannot at all agree with one writer who says that life and nature are made up of exceptions and that the exception is much more interesting than the rule which it breaks. Let us look the matter squarely in the face and I will boldly challenge the world to show me "exceptions" in Nature. Combinations we shall find in a stupefying profusion, but an exception, in the sense in which we mean it, never. As she loves variety, so she produces unexpected results by combining various forces, and while seemingly she deviates from the letter of her harmonic laws, yet she never in fact does so. The forces at work are so varied in their application that no one of

them is uninfluenced by the other. Half of our scientific instruments
are based on knowledge of this condition. The aneroid barometer
owes its usefulness to the fact that pressures differ at varying altitudes
and under differing conditions at the same altitude. Knowing then
her reliability, we have but to fathom her rules and the results are
certain. She combines with a dizzying readiness, *but* (and what a
but is this) Nature never forgets, never changes her mind, and, given
the same conditions, she will today produce with the most mathematical exactness the precise result with which she answered the same
conditions on that first day when the world was without form and
void.

Man meets this condition with a constant necessity for what,
for lack of a better term, I have designated as compensations, the
synthetic building up of combinations of influences which shall produce, in their co-operation, the result which he wishes to achieve. We
see this every moment of our lives, in the homeliest things and in the
arts as well. That this is true in music is well known and was shown
at some length in a previous work[1] where the deviation between what
would be a perfect chromatic scale and the accepted scale as in use
was explained,—a point familiar to every student of the subject of
"equalized temperament." Do we charge Pheidias with a lack of
knowledge governing the structure of the human body when he con-

[1] Appendix, Note XXIX and *Music in Nature* (Coan).

structed his famous Minerya in the contest with Alcamenes? Seeing the judges about to turn with disdain from his statue which they hastily condemned as uncouth and out of proportion, Pheidias, as you will recollect, asked them if it was not at the top of a column that the statue was intended to be placed, and when answered in the affirmative, he calmly informed them that it had been designed with that in view and asked that it be inspected *from that position*. Pheidias merely took the laws of optics into consideration and worked his subject so that, from its given position it should show to the observers exactly what he saw in his mind's eye and in the small statue from which it had been created.

Turning back then to plate 118 showing the Parthenon let us take into consideration the fact that of all classic architecture none more clearly indicates the government of the tetragon family. A descriptive correlation will clearly disclose that, if the figure be escribed in a circle measuring the length of the lowest step (that being the greatest measurement) then the immovable circle of the first progression will place the inner line of the outside columns, the line of the circle of the second progression will place the height of the peak of the raking cornice over the pediment (thus measuring the vertical extreme) and will place, as well, the base of the second pair of columns. The fourth circle places the entablature, the fifth the dentils and the metopes as well as the bases of the inner columns, the sixth measures their centres and the emplacement of the lower entablature, while the eighth defines the place of the inside base of the two inner columns.

Do we take it that all of these things are the result of mere "accidental coincidence" on the part of watchful Iktinus? Remember that these diagrammatic distances as measured by the progressive circles are fixed by geometry, and once the circumscribing circle is drawn, the architect has no more control of where the succeeding members will fall than has the reader. They come absolutely where calculation says they must, and always in the same place, regardless of whether that place suits the conclusions of the student or not.

Let us remember also, while we are on the subject, that these progressions of the square as here drawn, are the same ones which we have seen indicated as the measurements of Nature's forces and developed constantly in her formations, some of which it is true are invisible and could not have been known to Iktinus, but many of which were as well understood by the Greeks as by ourselves. It is unnecessary to assume that the ancients ferreted out and followed definite rules of Nature which we have since unearthed. It is quite sufficient that they are conceded to have followed the results which they saw on all hands with much more studious attention than do we.

Being now fairly under way on the subject of the adaptation by man of the rule and module of natural proportions, what better way is afforded of weighing the evidence and testing the proof than by look-

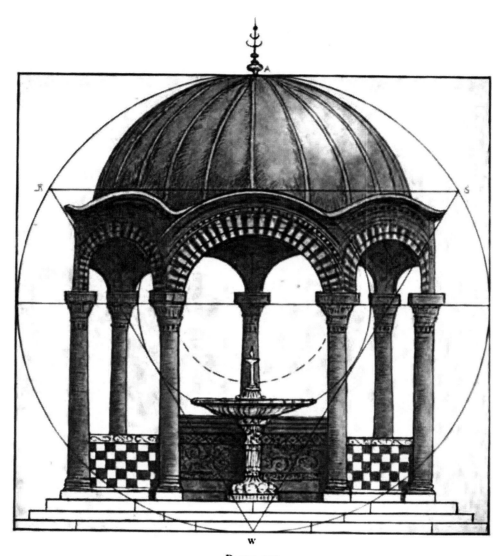

PLATE 119
DESIGN FOR A FOUNTAIN

PLATE 120

SAN GIOVANNI, SIENA

ing over specific cases. Of these we shall find in plate 119 a most graphic example of work designed on the same schedule as the Parthenon, to wit, the progression of the square and the equilateral triangle. In this it has not been thought necessary to insert all of the confusing lines of the web disclosed in plates 1 and 2, but if they are followed out, it will be noted that the correlations describe the entire figure. The triangle R S W outlines the cornice, and, where it intersects the triangle, apex upward (plate 2 A T V) on the middle horizontal, the point of juncture indicates the centre of the middle supporting column. The circle of the second progression clearly defines the spring of the central arch and these proportional coincidences continue throughout the figure. In plate 120, Church of San Giovanni, Siena, we see another most definite case of tetragonal proportioning in which the prime circle sets the width of the outside buttress columns, the second the centres of the intercolumnar spaces, the third the outside, and the fourth the inside of the inner buttress columns with great exactness.

That many of the finest old arches have been constructed on this basis is readily seen by a glance at plate 121, Arch of Augustus at Susa, plate 122, Arch of Titus at Rome, plate 123, the Arch of Augustus at Rimini, and plate 124, Arch of Augustus at Aosta. Correlating descriptions of these may, perhaps, be superfluous, but for the sake of stressing the point in hand it is not unwise to note that in all these examples of architecture of the Romans while still under Greek influence the progression of the square is plainly in evidence as in the Arch of Augustus at Aosta, where three progressions of the square

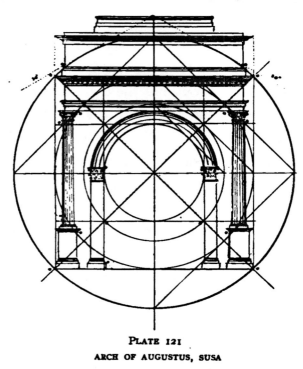

PLATE 121
ARCH OF AUGUSTUS, SUSA

produce the chief proportional spaces. The Arch at Susa as drawn in plate 121 discloses a similar influence as combining three progressions of the square. In this case the work is escribed by the rectangle of 45° to the top of the main cornice, the height of the attic being decided by the angle of 30° passing tangent to the primary circle. If the rectangle is divided into sixteen squares, these will render many of the proportional spaces, as at the points *o*.

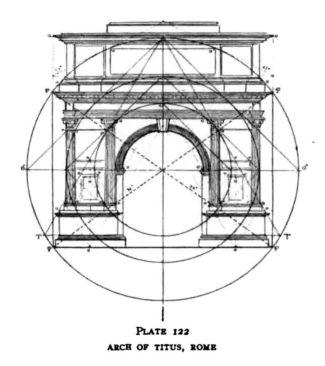

PLATE 122
ARCH OF TITUS, ROME

The Arch of Titus at Rome is now generally considered to be the finest of all of the triumphal arches in existence and is drawn at plate 122. Its beauty would seem to be largely achieved by the judicious use of some such principles as applied in the cases of the other arches, though perhaps with more intelligent originality. Three progressions of the square, coupled with one of the triangle of 60°, will be found upon examination to place its proportions. The placing of the main triangle of 60° and the smaller ones at its base is

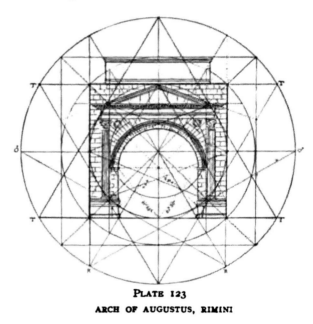

PLATE 123

ARCH OF AUGUSTUS, RIMINI

from Viollet-le-Duc, who in his *Discourses on Architecture* gives us numerous other examples of this triangle similarly applied. The correlations at the points *o* in this diagram are remarkable and should be carefully followed out. The Arch of Augustus at Rimini, plate 123, illustrates the same principle but with a pediment

above, the raking cornice of which is at an angle harmonic with the
plan.[1]

The subject of the use of the circle in proportions of its progressions as ordered by the square and the equilateral triangle would

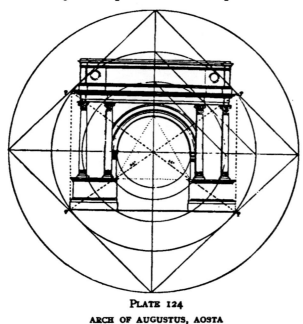

PLATE 124

ARCH OF AUGUSTUS, AOSTA

scarcely be complete without a reference to the symbol of the Royal
Arch Masons known as Solomon's Seal as shown in plate 125. The
real significance of this figure remained sealed in the minds of a very
few of the higher officers. Legends as to its meaning are rampant and

[1] *Nature's Harmonic Unity*, pp. 244, 251.

14

every man has a different one to tell, but the true significance was probably lost in the dark ages when masonry and the Knights Templars

PLATE 125
' SOLOMON'S SEAL AND THE ROYAL ARCH MASONS

for a time went actually out of being, or pursued their lives, forbidden of court and by law, in an underground existence of profound mysticism. The great interest attaching to the Seal of Solomon as here portrayed comes from the positive knowledge of its exceedingly great age. Not only does legend connect it with the days of our early ancestors, but the explorations in Uxmal within recent times have disclosed a temple at least three thousand years old, which conforms in every respect to the requirements of the rites of the order, and on the walls of which this symbol still shows its lines clearly to the eye of all comers.[1] It will be noticed that the upper circle is the first progression of that escribing the crossed triangles and forming interiorly the hexagon with which we have become so familiar in our study in the chapter on force. The inner of the two upper circles, together with the small one at the bottom, are all formed by the second progression of the same figure, and the small triangle is that of the fourth progression. While one is in no position to guess what might have been the original meaning, and with no intention to pass upon such as are at present attributed nor to delve into questions which the Masonic authorities wish to keep secret, it is nevertheless a matter of considerable interest to note that the ancients of so great antiquity were unquestionably able to construct not only progressing circles, triangles, and hexagons, but that they held certain of these figures in great reverence, and that these were intimately connected with the progressions which we have found laid down time after time by Nature in her constant demonstrations.

[1] Le Plongeon and Orestes Bean.

Many pieces of sculpture are expressed along similar lines, but space is insufficient to give them place. It is enough to call attention to the fact that where sculpture represents man singly, all that has been said about the canons for the measurement of the human body will be found to apply, and where sculpture is found in groupings of figures, which is infrequently the case, the group is susceptible of only two methods of treatment: either taken as a solid with its spaces both in perspective as well as lateral entering into consideration (in which case it presents questions too complex for vital study here), or viewed as a flat picture, in which case what is said in regard to pictures n general will apply. As an example of the latter method, one ought to give a moment to the contemplation of the group known contemporaneously as the "Farnese Bull" which is shown in plate 126 where Amphion and Zethus appear binding their mother's enemy, Dirce, to the horns of a wild bull. The manner in which from the observer's present point of view the figures pile up on one another in the central climax might have been the ideal of a geometer bent upon symbolising the equilateral triangle in marble or bronze.

The frequency with which architects have utilised the proportions of the tetragon family in apportioning their spaces is perhaps equalled in the number of times, especially in Gothic art, when the proportions are those of extreme and mean ratio. It is not perhaps amiss to call attention to this change. The Greeks, as has been shown

PLATE 126

FARNESE BULL

and might be amplified, used the square and the equilateral triangle almost exclusively in their buildings. Witness the Parthenon, as already
described, the Temple of Jupiter Panhellenius at Ægina, the Choragic
Monument of Lysicrates, and many others. In this the Romans
were prone to follow them, as seen in their arches as already depicted,

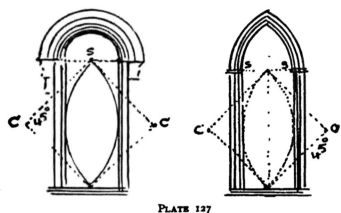

PLATE 127
VESICA PISCIS AND GOTHIC ARCH

and in the Basilica Constantine and many other examples. With
the upspringing of the Gothic form, and the greater variety and
flexibility of form came greater ability to use such an equally flexible
scale as that presented by extreme and mean ratio.

The meaning and construction and use of the vesica piscis, which
was the outgrowth of the two-focused arch, is shown in plate 127
from which it is possible to see something of the reason which lead

architects quickly to choose it in preference to the only iron-bound forms of which the barrel vaulting of its predecessors was capable.

Nor is it difficult to understand why the use of extreme and mean ratio and the golden series received an enormous impetus from the change from Norman architecture or Roman forms to the Gothic. There are good reasons for almost everything if only we have the patience to look for them and this is no exception to the rule. In the older schools the barrel vaulting called for fixed forms of window openings, and nearly fixed relations between all points where two systems of roofing or vaulting came into contact, as at the "lantern" of a great church or cathedral. Thus the relations between the nave and the aisles, between the aisles and the lantern, between the width of the nave and the size of the bays opening into it, were only partially within the discretion of the architect. Having chosen the circular form of arch with its one focus, that form demanded that its own plan be carried out through the whole, and the relations scientifically permitted between the various portions were largely prolific in the ratio of 2:4 and 3:4 but never permitted such a comparison as is expressed in the golden series. These, mind you, were not voluntary questions of decoration, but the ultimately fundamental builders' necessities of support, stress, and strength. As these fell naturally into the relations of the square and its progressions which so easily produce the equilateral triangle and the hexagon, as already seen, what was

more natural than that the architect should call on the decorated spaces for an ornamentation which was in keeping with his basic design?

Following the gradual adoption of the Gothic form with its two focused arches, in which widths of aisle and bay, arch and window were permitted to have pretty much such a relation to each other as the architect saw fit, the merit of the golden section, now available, naturally came into prominence: and we find it growing in favour as a module nearly in correspondence with the growth of the Gothic form. Many of the earlier cathedrals which still showed a disposition to indicate the relations of their parts and the shape of their minor units by the equilateral triangle nevertheless begin to make their grand divisions in accordance with the principles of extreme and mean proportion. Marked cases of this are the cathedrals of Amiens and Notre Dame in Paris. Viollet-le-Duc, who restored these magnificent buildings and was conversant with all of their parts, interior as well as exterior, furnishes convincing diagrams and shows in his analysis the unmistakable evidences of the continuous use of the golden series, [1] while the service of the equilateral triangle in minor decoration is well defined in plate 128 showing the west front of Amiens.

The facility with which the architect of the Middle Ages and his successors made the chief fronts of their buildings conform to the pro-

[1] Appendix, Note XXX.

portions of the golden series in many instances may easily be seen by a glance at the fronts of cathedrals such as Paris where the galleries and the towers and the windows and the buttressed spaces subdivide themselves repeatedly into these ratios, as we shall shortly see also in the case of Exeter. Again, as in plates 129 and 130, we see how frequently well-known buildings submit themselves perfectly to the dimensional rules of the pentagon and pentagram, as simply as an unfolding flower. Can we look at the portal of San Donnino of Emilia (plate 129) set in the pentagon, with the interior arches of the portal indicated by the succeeding circles of the progression, without feeling that by serious intent of the architect or by amazing accident on his part the creation conforms astonishingly to the rule as laid down? Then look at the portal of the Palazzo Publico, Perugia, in plate 130, and see the same principles applied in an entirely different way, but with equally certain results. The latter case is also worthy of note in that the spirals, which in most cases are sun-wise, will be found to turn against the sun in the series next but one on the right of the doorway.

Before proceeding to the examination of paintings, it would be well to look for a moment at plate 131 in which we shall find the asymmetrical spiral of the pentagon developed after the manner described by Mr. Church, as this is a most helpful device for placing the subdivisions of many famous paintings, as can be seen in its applica-

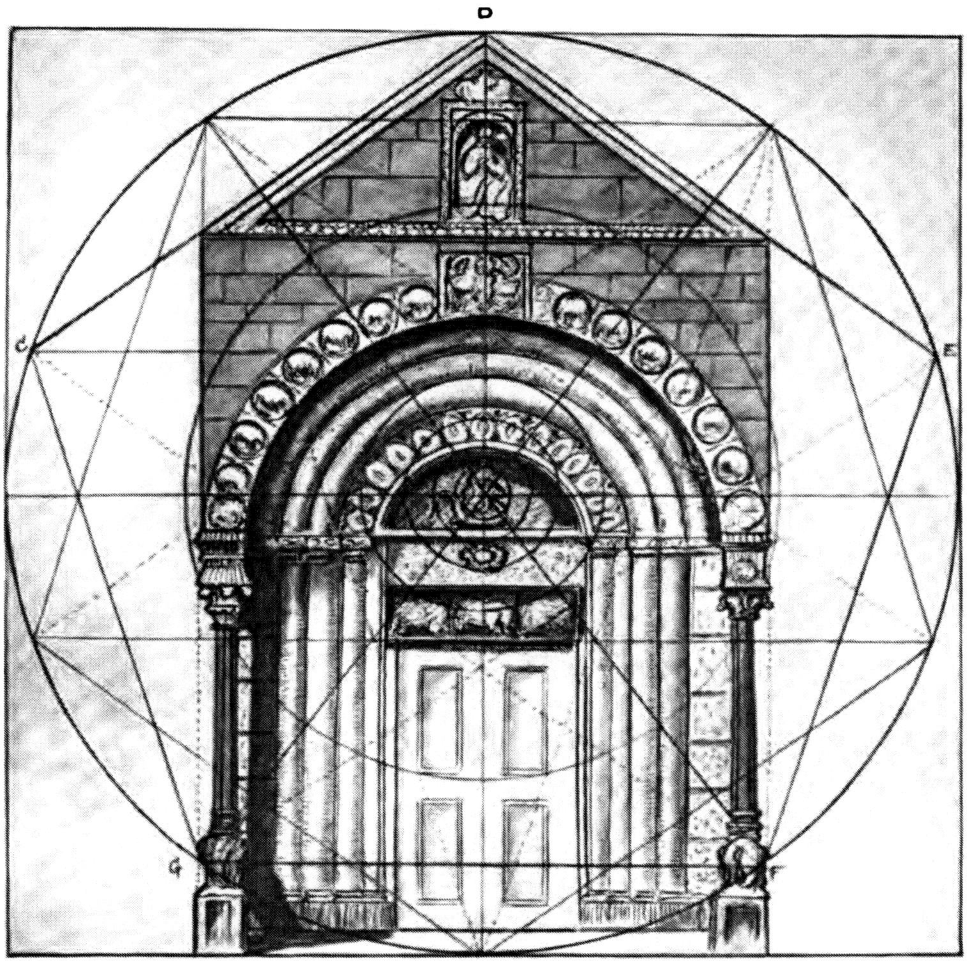

PLATE 129
PORTAL OF SAN DONNINO OF EMILIA

PLATE 130
PALAZZO PUBLICO, PERUGIA

tion. The lines of these asymmetrical spirals, springing from the centre, pass then through the apex of the pentagon of the third progression as at *x*, continuing through the raking slope of the prime figure as at *y*, that being the point of its intersection with the horizon-

PLATE 131

ASYMMETRICAL SPIRALS APPLIED TO THE PENTAGON (METHOD OF CHURCH)

tal of the same pentagon inverted, and then proceeds to the exterior point at Z. If we add to this descriptive correlation the fact that other curves of the same nature are drawn from all similar points, we shall have sufficiently described the plan to make it intelligible as a tool.

Applying these spirals and the pentagon to several famous paintings, we shall see that they place the artistic centre of the picture, besides furnishing an index of the positions of various figures, and a correlating description of each of the plates is here presented. In plate 132 we have the most famous of the works of Titian and by many thought to be the most beautiful painting in the world. Here, as in other cases, the proportions are decided by the pentagon united to the law of movement, with the golden series written at practically every intersection. The centre of the geometric plan makes the centre also of the picture, placing the positions of God the Father and of the Virgin, as well, while the curves of movement add many other points. In plate 133 we have a touch from the brush of Rubens in which the angels are delineated in a way permitting much the same description as before. Titian's *Entombment* is shown in plate 134, a work often condemned as lacking in some respects in drawing. It is of great interest, however, to note how the lines fall in with the centralization of the picture and how what are commonly nominated as errors of drawing tend (perhaps intentionally) to enhance the force and meaning of the group. In plate 135 Raphael's *Madonna of the Cradle* is shown, wherein even the slightest examination will disclose many examples of the use of something very akin to the golden series in apportioning of the spaces. Tintoretto's masterpiece appears in plate 136, the *Miracle of St. Mark*, with the patron saint of Venice whirling down from the clouds on one curve of movement, continued by the standing figure with the hammer, below, as well as that of the

PLATE 132
THE ASSUMPTION. TITIAN

PLATE 133
RUBENS'S ANGELS

PLATE 134
THE ENTOMBMENT—TITIAN

PLATE 135
MADONNA OF THE CRADLE—RAPHAEL

PLATE 136

PLATE 137
ANTIQUE EWER DESIGNED ON
AN ELLIPSE

PLATE 138
PHŒNIX DESIGN IN ECCENTRIC CIRCLES FROM AN
ANCIENT CHINESE RUG

prone slave and many of the other figures. All of these are but other forms of the law of movement as shown in the serrated edges of leaves and the curves of their veins as described in plates 52 and 53.

Turning, for the moment, to those forms which are asymmetric but not spiral, let us examine plate 137 in which we see the graceful outlines of an old ewer, each curve of which, like the loutrophoros in plate 60, is determined by the ellipse, even to the corrugations of the pattern. To this, in much the same spirit, might be added many beautiful old flagons and hammered brass pitchers did space but permit. Instead of these, we see in plate 138 another eccentric design, taken from an antique Chinese rug belonging once to the Bischoff collection and showing a graceful figure of the phœnix, in which each circumference of wing and tail feathers forms a circle eccentric to the others as explained in the plate numbered 61.

It is impossible to pass from the subject of rugs without mentioning some, at least, of the familiar border designs which have an important bearing upon all of the best of these. Of such patterns doubtless the most familiar is the Meander, which, I probably need not say, takes its name, like our own vague and winding stroll, from the little stream in Asia Minor which strives so hard, with many twistings, to reach the Ægean at Miletus. In all of the standard rugs we find many forms of the Meander and the "T" fret such as shown in plate 139, and these, in turn, easily lead into another frequently met design of the *svastika*, in various combinations, one of which is shown in plate 140 as it occupied the centre of a beautiful Ch'ien-lung rug of sapphire blue and pomegranate, making a wonderfully effective medallion.

It is interesting to note that the divisions of this figure, if the

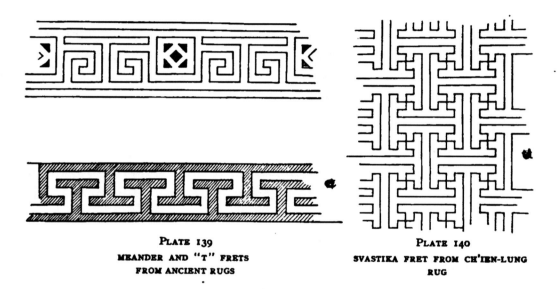

PLATE 139
MEANDER AND "T" FRETS
FROM ANCIENT RUGS

PLATE 140
SVASTIKA FRET FROM CH'IEN-LUNG
RUG

gammadion tradition be abandoned, lend themselves with peculiar nicety to the proportions of the golden series, and in plate 141 this continued relation of the extreme and mean ratio is depicted as governing both the figure and its intervening spaces, and should be compared with the design of a plane of the golden series in plate 5. It must not, however, be thought that there is any official or recognised rule for the proportions of the *svastika*, but merely that it lends itself so readily to the ratio in question.[1] Indeed, it will be frequently noted, as in plate 142, that these proportions do not obtain. It will be remembered that this four-legged outline has been held rather in awe and reverence, as already indicated, and foretells, if we may be-

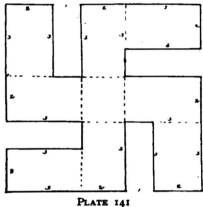

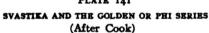

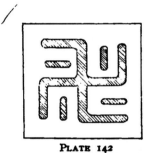

PLATE 141
SVASTIKA AND THE GOLDEN OR PHI SERIES
(After Cook)

PLATE 142
SVASTIKA IN COUNTER-SUN PATTERN, FROM A
SAXON CINERARY URN

lieve the credulous, good luck when it turns with the sun, and notably ill luck when the opposite is the case. To emphasise this, I have introduced the design of *svastika* taken from a Saxon cinerary urn, where the symbol is distinctly counter-sun, in a manner portentous and dread, doubtless conveying the symbolism of death itself.

---

[1] For further interesting facts and traditions concerning *svastika*, gammadion, and other ancient symbols, see Appendix, Note XXXI.

So far, we have viewed spirals as the result of growth or design, but naturally these forms may be assumed under almost any influence, and it is interesting to note that spirals beget spirals, even by physical reaction. It is recognised that in the laws of physics, action is to be followed by a reaction, which is equal in force and opposite in direction. Modifying this by the realising sense that a portion of the force is absorbed by the agent causing the reaction, we may accept the truth as indisputable and displayed every day. If we look in a

PLATE 143

REACTIONARY SPIRALS

mirror, we see it in the reflection, if we go to church, we hear it from the sounding board, if we play billiards, we learn it from both cushion and ball, the gun fires its projectile but has a recoil which must be taken into account, and so it goes on continually. Put this now into our category of things to be examined and see how it effects the spiral tendency. Our forbears, wishing to make a large cord out of a small one, twisted it into a spiral until it was ready to kink. Then if the two ends were brought together and the middle bight suddenly dropped, do we remember what would happen? The released cord, of course, reacted on itself and formed a new spiral with so much tenacity that it would stay in that form indefinitely. This is illustrated in plate 143, and may be examined well in connection with the other spirals shown earlier. It is not to be confused with the natural

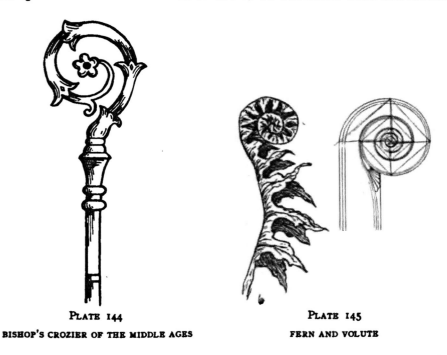

PLATE 144

BISHOP'S CROZIER OF THE MIDDLE AGES

PLATE 145

FERN AND VOLUTE

tendency of a spiral vine to twine back on itself in the absence of other support, if turned downwards. This latter is merely an example of the willingness of a loosened branch to twine upwards on anything, even on itself, while in the instance we have shown, the loosened cord would curl back on no unsympathetic outside element, but only on its straining other self.

Under this head one ought not to fail in calling attention, trite as it may be, to the beautiful similarity, already noted under begonia, between the fern, the Ionic volute, and the crozier of my Lord Bishop. In plate 144 we have a drawing of a Bishop's crook of the Middle Ages and, in order to facilitate the comparison, in plate 145 the fern and the volute. [1]

Not alone in Greece and classic lands can we expect to find beautiful evidences of the golden series. T'ai-tsung may have headed an unfortunate dynasty in the far eastern land which he called Chin or T'sin and which his children's children learned to hear called Cathay after his best hated enemy, the Khitan, but notwithstanding all of these myriad misfortunes, industry and art furnished in the reign of the Tsung dynasty many things of beauty, some of which have come down to us today. Amongst these is the tea bowl shown in plate 146, and, strange as it may seem, this pottery design follows the line of extreme and mean proportion with a fidelity truly remarkable. Let us study its correlations and set down a short description of its lines. If we draw a circle with the radius K C, it will pass enscribing the lip of the bowl at A and E. If now, another circle be drawn with the radius C D so that it touches the lip at the central

[1] Appendix, Note XXXII.

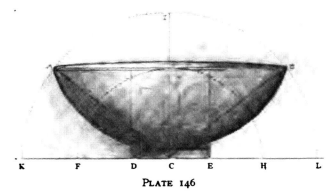

| K | | F | | D | C | E | | H | | L |

PLATE 146

TEA BOWL OF THE TSUNG DYNASTY, SHOWING THE GOLDEN SERIES

PLATE 147

ELEANOR GRILL, WESTMINSTER

PLATE 148
STAINED GLASS BORDER IN SPIRALS, FROM
CANTERBURY
(Day)

PLATE 149
ST. KIMBERT'S BORDER, COLOGNE (Day)

point, it will be found to cut the radius CI into an extreme and mean proportion. Taking a step farther, by measuring the base from the centre at C to the edge of the foot at D, we find that we have established a perfect golden series, in which all the terms are in proportion.

The beauties of these varied curves and proportions meet endless exemplification, but nowhere more markedly than in the art of the iron-worker (for we had our Quentin Matsys, remember) and the glass painter, the silversmith, and the wood-carver. In Westminster one remembers with pleasure the wonderful touches of Grinling Gibbons, and along with them many a screen of wrought iron. That protecting the tomb of Queen Eleanor and called the "Eleanor Grill" is shown in plate 147. This exquisite piece of workmanship was designed by Thomas de Legton in the thirteenth century, contains many interesting flat spirals, and is as fine an example of metal work as could well be found.

The charming works in stained glass painting are so seldom claimed by students of the arts that it is a pleasure to examine one or two borders from Day's *Windows*. In plate 148 we have a border from Canterbury, plentiful in spirals, and in plate 149 a drawing of St. Kimbert's border at Cologne. Both will repay study of any searcher in the realm of spirals, as will the handles and the band decorations of the Ampulian amphora shown in plate 150, on which scenes from Euripides' Hecuba are shown, and which has been so well

15

described at length by H. B. Walters, keeper of Greek antiquities in the British Museum.

No writer who referred even remotely to the subject of spirals could, of course, be excused for omitting, in the long run, to mention the great spiral staircases to be found scattered over the continent of Europe. Not being possible to show more than one of these, I have chosen to wander again in Venice. Dispensing with guide and gondola, ferry or sandola, we will stroll through the Piazza, and Via Ventidue Marzo, passing by the bridge to the Academy where we left Titian's Assumption but a brief moment ago, and so on up to the right past San Stefano, making our way as roundabout as can well be, in order to get into the quiet spirit of ancient Venice, before we bring up at the Corte del Maltese and the beautiful winding stairway of the Contarini del Bovolo. What a day it was for the world when the Contarini and the Minelli and the doge and the prince thought it nothing unusual to decorate their palaces exteriorly, as in this case, so that all was not lost within four dour walls. Of all of the spiral stairways, this, patterned, it has been suggested, after some remote ancestor of the shell scalaria scalaris appeals to me as being the most easily understood when studied as a spiral, and it, therefore, is the one which has been offered for examination. Leonardo's world wonder at Blois will repay a life study, as would many another, but we must needs pass on to things other than these, for our little day is nearly up.

PLATE 150

ANCIENT AMPHORA OF THE AMPULIAN
ORDER. HANDLES AND BAND DECO-
RATION IN SPIRALS

PLATE 151

WINDING STAIRWAY OF PALAZZO
CONTARINI DEL BOVOLO

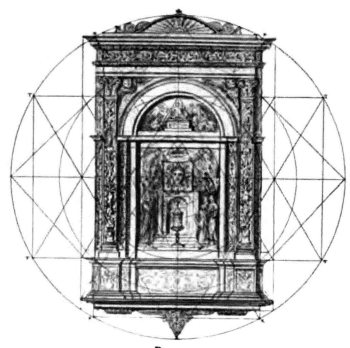

PLATE 152

DESIGN FOR TABERNACLE FOR THE SACRED OIL

To touch once more on the tetragon family before leaving to the reader the entire subject, let us examine the drawing shown in plate 152 of a design in the web of the equilateral triangle for a Tabernacle

PLATE 153

CLOISTERS OF ST. JOHN LATERAN SHOWING VARIOUS COLUMNAR SPIRALS

of the Sacred Oil in the style of the Italian Renaissance and we shall envisage the ease with which these rules lend themselves to design. Then, turning quickly to plate 153 we shall be prepared the better to understand the quiet cloisters of St. John Lateran, where one may give time properly to examine the countless things of beauty, not least of which are the spiral columns in a bewildering variety. They seem to vie with each other in their differences, as the sun plays hide-and-seek with the shadows and the reflections in the old well-head in the centre. Cool the court is and green and we may well be thankful that "round the cool green courts there runs a row of cloisters" since the cloisters hold for us so much of interest. Our spirals are types of Nature's power, types of man's accomplishment, types, who knows, of the greatest Power of all, for the worship of whom this quiet spot is set apart.

We have said that the cathedrals of the Middle Ages frequently showed a division in height and width in exact relation to the golden series, and in keeping with the proportional allocation of the parts of the human body. Let us then examine plate 154, a drawing of the west front of Exeter. Here we shall see that the distance between the top of the screen of niches on the west front and the line marking the top of the aisles furnishes us the first step in a continuing golden series as laid out in the space marked "A" on the scale below. This, in turn, gives place to "B," which measures the height of the screen from the ground. The sum of these, which is the next term, shows the clerestory as from II to IV on the side spaces or unit "D" on the scale, completing the entire height of the

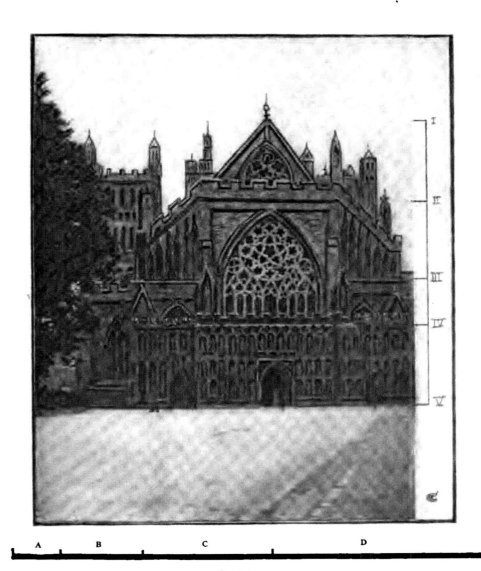

PLATE 154

WEST FRONT OF EXETER CATHEDRAL, SHOWING DIVISION INTO THE GOLDEN SERIES

front in a serial order which will be found to repeat itself in many other proportions.

Writing, alas, on such a subject partakes distinctly of the nature of the golden series itself: there is always another step in sight which might well be taken. Not infrequently this other step, continuing the analogy, seems as the greater quantity in comparison as past accomplishment seems too often the less. Desire and ambition and material would carry us on and on indefinitely, but, since our golden series is itself indefinitely continuous, so must we make a period both in illustration and in argument. I, for one, shall not despair that a point has been scored, however much must inevitably be left undone. Perhaps we may be permitted to think that something worth while has been said; and happy he would be who writes, digresses, and writes again, if in the end, viewing his work as did John Skelton so long ago, he may say,

> Though my ryme be ragged,
> Tattered and jagged,
> Rudely rayne-beaten,
> Rusty and moughte eaten,
> *It hath in it some pyth.*

CHAPTER VIII

THE TAG

EVERY dramatist, be he at the top of the profession or the most lowly amateur that ever trod the boards in fear and trembling, has a certain kinship in one thing,—his persistent and superstitious horror of speaking the last few words of the play or epilogue, the tag, so called, in any rehearsal or under any circumstances, until the actual performance at its first presentation is complete. It will be recognised that what the moral is to a fable, the tag is to the play, and premature speaking of the tag is to bring down all of the evil luck of stagedom upon one and to mark the unlucky wight as the most ignorant and the most forgetful of his tribe.

It is presumed that every writer has his purpose, and in this we plead no difference from the next. The work is finished, the play is done, and the curtain is about to fall. Hence the epilogue must be spoken e'er it be too late.

Daily, every work which dares attempt to seek out the source of beauty is met by the scoffing challenge that Beauty is kin to Good Taste and that the twain are beings so tenuous that a mere breath of inspection will blow them completely away to that terra incognita where they join hands with Inspiration and roam at will, defying man to catch them and only coming out to smile at him at their own good pleasure, then to disappear and leave him again disconsolate.

According to this view it is a near-sacrilege to pry into the origin of an inspired work of the muses or of the brush or pen, and as to laying down rules for any of these three partners! Perish the thought, and likewise, perish the thinker. And it is a bold writer who will confront this prejudice.

Now, I am far from saying that beauty can only be attained in art and architecture and music and poetry and painting by the aid of the rules here or anywhere yet laid down, nor that such rules are any substitute for inspiration or creative genius. What, however, I do say and say positively is that there is no such thing as beauty or good taste, nor will there ever be, which does not conform to rules and laws, many of them strictly mathematical. We may not, at the time, know the specific rule or combination of rules governing the production and which make it beautiful, but sooner or later, if the taste be good and the work truly worthy, the reason will come to us, as the reason that the chords formed on the diatonic scale are agreeable has come through scientific knowledge centuries after Pythagoras discovered the bare fact that they were so. Are they any the less beautiful now that we know that a reason exists for the beauty?

Were they, to be consistent, more beautiful before Pythagoras learned even so much as he disclosed about them? Can any one point to any single thing of beauty in the entire universe, concerning which, when we came to investigate it and understand it, there did not appear a rational basis upon which rules could be built?

No, there is no claim made that beauty must all be upon the rules of the game as already discovered and laid down, but merely that *all beauty must be according to some rules, discovered or discoverable.* Science has far from reached the limit of its disclosures, and beauty, too, may go on and on for generations, through which every new development of the beautiful will warrant the closest examination of its causes, with the same careful scrutiny that would follow a development of the unknown in Natural phenomena.

Since, then, admittedly, new rules may develop, why, perhaps you inquire, need we study the old ones? If you ask that question I can only compare it to a soldier going into battle. He knows that any day a new explosive may be built up in the laboratories of his own or the enemy's scientists, but does this prevent him from insisting on having his full supply of the best that has been devised to the date of the contest? Every new law of science then will be a new road to beauty and every new inspiration to beauty will disclose new laws upon which it is based.

The voice most dissonant to all of these conclusions will doubtless be found belonging to someone who anxiously allows his boy or girl to spend valuable hours of study and expensive weeks of travel in order to become acquainted with the best there is in the world,—the best in literature, the best in sculpture, the best in music, and the best in architecture. And all for what? Is this expenditure of time and strength for the mere idle pleasure of adulation,—the bowing down before the master and his masterpiece? No, you say, it is as a matter of education. If the beautiful be, perchance, this effervescent thing based solely upon an inspired stroke and defiant of every rule and restraint, how, then, will study of such a flash-in-the-pan serve to educate? Why stop to inspect the structure of that which lacks the fundamental rules of construction? Is beauty, indeed, thus *non compos mentis?* Without reason, analogies are lost: without reason and analogies, study is a vain thing. No, deep down in our inner consciousnesses we one and all know perfectly that a reason exists for all beauty and it is only our human stupidity which prevents us from ascertaining what that reason is,—and largely the delusion that beauty and inspiration are borne of the mists of unreason has been the explanation of our failure to progress faster and farther than we have.

If then we do not study the masters and their masterpieces merely as a semi-religious rite, what, pray, is the purpose unless it be to learn how they did them. Do we then argue that this set of rules which we hope to derive from the examination of these splendid works arose triumphant from the very thing itself, once accomplished, having had no existence beforehand? This reason which we hope to pin down, was it no factor in the success of the master in creating his masterpieces? If it will help us to know, did it not then help him likewise to create? And if so, into what thin air does the plea against rule and reason as applied to beauty dissolve.

The purpose of it all then is that we may improve, and expand, and so far as the writers of the present book are concerned (now here is spoken the tag) it is the labour of hope,—the hope that it may help both ourselves and others not merely to understand and appreciate, but also, perhaps, to be creators of

Things of Beauty.

APPENDIX NOTES

INTRODUCTORY

It is frequently conceived that, if one writing on a definite topic, fills his pages with his chosen subject, he does so in the conviction that nothing else equally important exists. Of any spirit akin to this, we emphatically plead not guilty. Equally illogical is the occasional critic who questions the merit of any research where the publication is by necessity limited to the propounding and substantiation of a given theory, unless all the bibliography which could conceivably bear on the subject is quoted copiously.

The purpose of this work is the presentation of certain interesting relations between the laws of Nature and the fundamentals of beauty, and so to present these that readers unacquainted with abstruse mathematical formulæ may find the path. Brevity is therefore important, and were all of the works which have been consulted enumerated here, the mere review would crowd out all else. Every good library presents such standard works as Haeckel, Schimper, Tyndall, and the numberless others familiar to the reading world, and after all is said and done, the acid test still remains. If a work contains something new and true, it justifies itself, whether couched in the language of exact science, as some would choose, or presented in the plain tongue of the people; and in advancing our arguments, which are in their nature somewhat specialized, these things have been kept in view.

Note I

For clarity, the relations of the sides and radii are here set out in percentages of the prime radius. It is unnecessary to furnish trigonometrical proof of most of the statements and it would be extremely pedagogic to indulge in such a waste as the particular statements in this note are largely based on calculations long recognised and in constant use, the chief features of which will be found in any reputable engineering tabulations.

The position of the first progression will be fixed by the measure of the radius of its inscribed circle, which may be learned from any standard reference to be Rad. .70710678; or the reader may easily figure this for himself, since the diagonal of the square in its first progression is obviously twice the radius of the prime circle. It follows that the diagonal is an hypothenuse equal to Rad. 2.0000, and that either side must be the square root of one half of the square of 1.0000, or the square root of .5000, which will be found to be, as before, .70710678.

By the same process, the position of the square in the second progression will be found to be fixed in terms of the prime radius, at .5000000.

The square in its second progression is therefore exactly octant to the prime position.

Referring to plate 1 we may summarise as follows:

Radius BO = .7071 of Radius AO
Radius CO = .5000 of Radius AO
Radius DO = .3535 of Radius AO
Side EF   = 1.414 of Radius AO
Side IJ   = Radius AO (*i.e.* I. J. is 1.414 of BO and BO is .7071 of AO. BO is therefore 1.414 of .7071 = 1. of AO)

Side MN   = Radius BO
Diameter EH = Twice Radius AO
Diameter IL = Twice Radius BO
Diameter MQ = Twice Radius CO and hence
Diameter IL = 2 x .7071 or 1.414 of AO, and
Diameter MQ = 2 x .5000 or 1. of AO
    Comparing this with above, we find:
Diameter IL = Side EF
Diameter MQ = Side IJ, etc.

For convenience, I append here the positions of the various progressions of the square, equilateral triangle, hexagon, and octagon, in terms of the prime radius, so that they may readily be compared.

Number	Equilateral Triangle	Square	Hexagon	Octagon
Prime	1.00000000	1.00000000	1.00000000	1.0000000
1	.50000000	.70710678	.8660254	.92388
2	.25000000	.50000000	.7500000	.853553
3	.12500000	.35355339	.6495180	.788583
4	.06250000	.25000000	.56250000	.728553
5	.03125000	.17677669	.4871390	.67309
6	.01562500	.12500000	.4218750	.621859
7	.00781250	.08838834	.3653540	.574523
8	.00390625	.06250000	.3164070	.53079
9	.00195312	.04419417	.274010	.49038
10	.00097656	.03125000	.237305	.45306

Note II

A mere glance at the tabulation set forth in note I will show that the radius of the first progression of the equilateral triangle and the radius of the second progression of the square are identical in position, each being fifty per cent. of the prime radius. A slight geometrical knowledge or a further glance at any standard tabulation will serve to assure that the side of the hexagon is the same length as the radius of the circle which inscribes it: thus AO and AR in plate 2 are identical in length with AO and IJ in plate 1.

Note III

Reference to Notes I and II will disclose that the following are all equal:

(RA) The side of the hexagon;
(AO) The radius of the prime circle;
(IJ) Side of the square in its second progression;
(MQ) Diagonal of the square in its third progression.

Since the radii CO in plate 1 and CO in plate 2 are each of them 50% of AO in the same plates, it follows that the lines IJ (side of the square in second progression) and RS (side of the equilateral triangle) lie in the same position and coincide. We may thus summarise as follows:

$$AO = EO = IJ = AR;$$
$$EF = IL;$$
$$EB = BO = MN;$$
$$MQ = IJ = AO = RT;$$
$$OC = CA = CJ;$$
$$OD = DB = MD;$$
$$MO = EM = OP = PG;$$
IJ   and RS fall on the same line;
KL   and TV fall on the same line;
IK   and JL would coincide with equilateral triangles drawn upright.

This, it is thought, will be sufficient to point the argument. Endless other coincidences will be observed by those who look for them, geometrically.

Note IV

The question for solution becomes this: what is the diagonal of a cube erected on the square IJKL in plate 2. This requires a double process for solution.

(1st) Ascertain the length of the diagonal of the square itself, since this is the base of the triangle on which is formed the new diagonal of the cube.

Taking the radius AO of our prime circle at the value of 1.00000 we have already found that the sides IJ and JL are equal to AO and, further, that the diameter IL equals the side EF, which, in turn is 1.414 of the radius AO. Hence it follows, that the diagonal IL measures 1.414 of the side IJ. We may confirm this for ourselves if we choose, by remembering that the square of the hypothenuse equals the square of the other two sides, which we know are of the value of 1.00 each. Hence, $\sqrt{\overline{IJ}^2 + \overline{JL}^2} = \sqrt{1^2 + 1^2} = \sqrt{1 + 1} = \sqrt{2} = 1.4142136$

(2d) The diagonal IL (plate 1, 2, or 3) has therefore the value in decimals of 1.414 of the side IJ or the radius AO and upon this we construct the triangle

LIS (plate 3), in which the side IS (or RS) forms the diagonal of the cube. Since the side IL has the ascertained value of 1.414 and the side LS is one of the edges of a cube valued at 1.00, we have the decimal value of the true diagonal of the cube shown by the equation:

$$\sqrt{\overline{IL}^2 + \overline{LS}^2} = \sqrt{1.4142136^2 + 1^2} = \sqrt{2 + 1} = \sqrt{3} = 1.7320508$$

the solution of which shows 1.7320508 as a result. Consulting now our reliable tabulation on engineering, we need not work out the length of one side of an equilateral triangle inscribed in a circle with a radius of the value of 1.00, since, without this trouble, we shall find that this side of our triangle, shown by the line RS in plates 2 and 3, has a value of 1.7320508, exactly coinciding with the value of the diagonal of the cube.

Note V

(A) Since the publication of *Nature's Harmonic Unity* several years ago, Sir Theodore A. Cook, in his most valuable and beautiful book *The Curves of Life*, has again taken up the subject of spirals, and, as an incident, touches repeatedly on various points relative to extreme and mean proportion, for which he has chosen the term "phi" (ϕ).

The great benefit to be derived from adopting a designation less cumbersome than the repetition of such a phrase as "continuous extreme and mean proportion" is obvious, but to my mind, only eventual confusion could result from the choice of the symbol ϕ. Its merit would lie in its brevity and the pretty and poetic fancy with which Sir Theodore connects it with the memory of Pheidias. Its fault, it seems to me, lies in the constant and earlier use of this Greek character, with quite well-defined and recognised association, in other and already occupied fields, amongst which need be only mentioned that of functions, where it appears repeatedly in such papers as the spherical harmonies of Laplace and the works of Lord Kelvin and others. Without theta and phi, one would be lost in this zone, nor is it the only one which might be called to attention.

One may, nevertheless, be not only brief but clear as well, in choosing the name "golden" to express this continuous series of extreme and mean proportion wherever it is found,—in the numerical or decimal form, in the linear, the circular,

16

the plane, the solid, or the spiral. Nor is such choice lacking in the classic touch which Sir Theodore would give to phi, since the earliest recognition of this ratio comes to us from the ancient days when it was known as the *Golden Section*. To this association I feel bound to adhere.

(*B*) Having already been emphasised in *Nature's Harmonic Unity*, it need hardly be amplified here, that this perfect and continuous golden series is of much greater importance than the mere bald division of a given unit into extreme and mean ratio. In the former work this was shown in many connections; in all pentamerous forms, page 295, in phyllotaxis, at page 312, in the series itself, as continuous at page 287 and 288, in the human anatomy at pages 181 *et seq.*, and in numerous other respects which need not be repeated here. It is valuable to note that the argument receives confirmation in *The Curves of Life*, further reference to this point being found in Note XXVII.

(*C*) At page 312 and elsewhere of *Nature's Harmonic Unity* I showed, I thought, quite definitely, the coincidence between the circular equivalent of extreme and mean proportion and the botanical "ideal angle," there claiming attention to the greater accuracy of the golden series than any possible application of the Fibonacci, for the measurement of growth, size, distance, or any feature other than mere numbering of parts; and it is interesting to note that the writer of *The Curves of Life*, while by inference supporting Dr. Church's explanation of Fibonacci in connection with his particular subject (as who could not where integers are possible) adds his conclusion that in other forms of natural growth it appears likely to give greater accuracy than the Fibonacci, and further suggests that research into its uses will be well repaid.

(*D*) My reason for calling this related curve the Golden Spiral is obvious, it being developed from the Golden Series. In *The Curves of Life*, already referred to, it is termed by the author the "phi" spiral, growing out of the same series, which, as explained before, he has termed the "phi"; a designation, which for reasons before presented, I am unable to follow and do not feel warranted in assisting to perpetuate.

Note VI

It is stated (1) That the angle formed by diagonal of a golden rectangle is 58° 16' and 17"; (2) that the decimal length of the diagonal of the golden rectangle is 1.175571 of the greater side, and (3) that the angle at the base of a golden solid is 54°, the same as that of the pentagon.

(1)   In proving the first proposition, let us form such a golden rectangle as that in plate 5, where AB represents the lesser side, to which we shall give the golden decimal value of .61803399, and AO the greater side, which will then have the value of 1.00, and the intervening angle known to be one of 90°.

AO + AB = 1.61803399 and AO − AB = .38196601, hence

1.61803399 : .38196601 :: Tang. 45°: Tang. ½ angles B − O

Log. 1.61803399   = 0.208988, ar. c. =   9.791012
Log. of .38196601 =   − 1.582024
Log. 45° Tang.   =   10.
                                              _____
value of result   9.373036
Angle of which this is log. tang. is 13° 16' 57"
which, added to half the sum or 45°
gives us 58° 16' 57" as the angle.

(2)   The length of the diagonal may be arrived at via the *pons assinorum*, as in Note IV since $\sqrt{\overline{AB}^2 + \overline{AO}^2}$ = diagonal BO (Plate 6). The logarithm of 1.38196601, which is the sum of these squares, is 0.140497. Dividing this by two to extract the square root, we have .070249, which, it will be found is the logarithm of 1.175571. The same result will, of course be obtained by the use of the customary proportion Sin B : Sin O :: 1 : x, since both angles are now known.

(3)   Having now developed the necessary factors of the triangle OBD in which the hypothenuse BD is the true diagonal of the golden solid, a similar process produces 54° as the angle.

Note VII

To form some inferential knowledge of the fourth dimension, even from an argumentative standpoint, let us begin on a foundation of recognised facts. A point, in mathematics, is that which hath position but no dimensions. If a point be moved straight forward, a line is formed; if this line be shoved sidewise at right angles to itself, we describe a plane surface; if the plane be raised upwards at right angles to its outlining sides, we form a cube or rectangle,—a solid. Here we stop, so far as human comprehension goes, with its call for visible demonstrations; but what, logically, would happen if a cube were moved at right angles to its own bounding sides? You say that this is impossible, since it would have to move in at least six directions at once. I grant you, it is impossible so far as we can *see*. Position, as we have said, requires no dimensions. One dimension is shown in length, two in length and breadth, three in solids having length, breadth, and thickness. Now in what form will a figure of four dimensions show itself? The reply is difficult to formulate, yet, mathematically, we can conceive the four as easily as we can evolve a fourth power of x—and that is just as simple as to form a cube. As Bragdon says: "With the geometry of such a space mathematicians long have been familiar, but is there such a space—is there any body for this mathematical soul? Adventure with me down a precipice of thought," says he, "sustained only by the rope of analogy, slender but strong. This rope, anchored in the firm ground of sensuous preception, extends three paces in the direction of the great abyss, then vanishes at the giddy brink. Let us examine this sustaining simile foot by foot and strand by strand. Familiar both to mind and eye are the space systems of one, two, and three dimensions; that is, lines, planes, solids. Lines are bounded by points, and themselves bound planes; line-bound planes in turn bound solids. *'What, then, do solids bound?'* Here is where the analogical rope vanishes from sight. If you answer that a solid cannot be a boundary, we part company. No argument of mine can convince you to the contrary. But if you are interested enough to ask, 'Well, what *do* solids bound?' logic compels the answer, *'Higher* solids; four dimensional forms (invisible to sight) related to the solids we know as are these related to their bounding planes, as planes to their bounding lines.'"

It is as simple to conceive all of this from a mathematical standpoint as it is to write an equation in the fourth power which shall be to the tessaract, a symbol as fitting as is the quadratic to the familiar plane. I cannot, however, hope to interest the readers of this work in any side subjects here, but would merely pause to state that at some later time it is my hope to show the intimate bearing of the golden series on the question of a fourth dimension, and to demonstrate that as the golden series is perfect and continuous, so it applies to all we know of fourth dimensional spaces as readily as it does to those more familiar to the world.

Note VIII

Perfect golden series as exemplified in the pentagon and pentagram.

The remarkable coincidences between the members of the pentagon and pentagram on the one hand, and the golden series on the other were demonstrated so fully in *Nature's Harmonic Unity*, at pages 297 to 305, that I hesitate to reintroduce these proofs which, being mathematical and demonstrably correct down to the seventh position of decimals, have never been challenged. Let us, for the purpose of this work, concede the statements as true, and, if desired, refer to the previous work for a demonstration.

Note IX

The sentence preceding this note, is one portion quoted from *Nature's Harmonic Unity*, beginning with the first reference to the ideal angle, and has been repeated here to emphasise the importance of this application of the golden angle or circular equivalent of the golden series. The last paragraph, written some eight or nine years ago, may well be considered in connection with the faith in extreme and mean proportion voiced in Note V (C).

Note X

When I restrict the polyhedra to these five, reference is strictly confined to the Platonic Regular Bodies. For the purposes of such a work as this, too great complications are presented when we turn to such figures as stellated or unwrapped polyhedra, inclosing the center more than once (as the great tetrahedron) and semi-regular bodies such as the tetrahexahedron, where all summits are alike but the plane angles vary. Even in the absence of such reasons as are contained in the text, these alone would be sufficient for the exclusion of all but the original five from consideration.

Note XI

It is but natural that decoration should follow and subdivide structural lines. Thus in the diatom, the snow crystal and the echinoderm, we find, where the structure is based on the square, the decoration immediately inclines to octagons; where the outlines are triangular, the decoration is hexagonal; and where the form is pentagonal, the decorated spaces will be found distributed according to the golden series. This, we shall see later, is true even in larger matters, the Norman style of architecture developing the circle, the square and their attributes, while the Gothic naturally lives in the *vesica piscis*, the traceried window, and other combinations possible but incongruous with the severity of the square and the triangle. So it is with other forms, but when structural density and tensile strength are questions of importance, then the hexagon comes into its own. On this subject Note XII should be consulted.

Note XII

On the subject of the formation of the bee's cell, the chief dispute seems to be, not, whether the six-sided cell is built to advantage, but as to whether or no, the bee deliberately and instinctively makes it hexagonal or simply forms it around her body and this form, under pressure, assumes hexagonal shape. There has, of late, been a good deal of argument on this subject. Mr. Bigelow, Dean Coulter, and Professor Gorton taking the negative and men of equal standing the affirmative. To my mind, this academic wrangle is powder wasted, since the result is inevitably a Scotch verdict, and the crucial question is, not whether the bee makes a circle which becomes a hexagon under certain influences favouring her needs, nor whether she forms it directly and by instinct, but whether, in the final analysis, she gets what she needs: (A) The greatest storage capacity without waste of space; (B) the greatest structural strength without waste of comb, and (C) the combination of the first two needs with a symmetry which shall fit her body and make her storing both possible and rapid.

Valuable notes on both the structural capacity of the bee's cell and also on the Reaumur-Miraldi legend will be found in the excellent work on *Growth and Form*, recently come from the pen of D'Arcy Thompson of University College, Dundee. In referring to the latter work, Colonel Millis (*Science*, October, 1918), writes more than interestingly on the subject of symmetric concentration. Experimenting with spheres, Colonel Millis goes to some length to support his statement that there is no arrangement possible giving both maximum density and universal symmetry. The cubical form propounded by him is perfectly symmetrical but reaches far from the maximum density. To offset this, he arranges a figure on angles of 116° 34′ and 54″ where the combination of density and symmetry is greatest, but concedes that *only in a rhombic form based on the hexagon is the maximum of density reached*. The descriptions are long but interesting and should be read at first hand, space not permitting their quotation here.

Note XIII

That the orbits of the planets coincided trigonometrically with the conditions presented in plates 38 and 39 was demonstrated in *Nature's Harmonic Unity* with sufficient detail to render further proof mere surplussage. Where so many points call for explanation and support, it is unwarranted, it would seem, to take up a second time proofs which have remained unchallenged through several years.

Note XIV

Measured in astronomical units, the variation between Bode's law and the distances as recited in any reliable table would show facts about as follows:

Planet	Dist. by Bode's Law	Actual Distance in Ast. Units	Variance in A. U.	Variance in miles approx.
Mercury	.4	.387	.013	1,200,000
Venus	.7	.723	.02	1,800,000
Earth	1.0	1.0	.00	module
Mars	1.6	1.52	.08	7,440,000
Jupiter	5.2	5.20	neg.	negligible
Saturn	10.0	9.53	.47	44,000,000
Uranus	19.6	19.19	.41	38,000,000
Neptune	38.8	30.00	8.80	very great

In spite of which, Bode's Law was the means of locating the asteroids, and partly responsible for the finding both of Uranus and Neptune.

Note XV

The three laws concerning light, sound, and gravity in the connection here stated are the fundamental basis of all investigation in the subjects referred to. They may be found stated in any authority on physics

Note XVI

If the reader will have the patience now to glance at the tabulation which I have compiled to illustrate these facts (see plate 43), he will instantly see why the tonic, mediant, dominant, and octave concur in the long recognized triad or "common chord," and why the tonic, subdominant, sixth, and tonic are also agreeable, and why the dominant and subdominant, each of which accords or harmonizes with the tonic, are discordant when sounded together. All of these statements are true, all are in absolute keeping with our theory based upon the coincidence of vibrations, and all are deducible with perfect clearness from our tabulation. An instant's examination shows that the tonic, mediant, dominant, and octave (constituting the common chord), *all* concur on every fourth wave-beat, or on lines, 1, 4, 8, etc., in the tabulation, the dominant and tonic meanwhile having made additional concurrences and the tonic and octave still others, so that in this common chord, in every four vibrations of the tonic there will be one wave-coincidence of the mediant, two of the dominant, and four of the octave. Could result ever follow theory more closely, or be more mathematically perfect?

Expending now a moment on the inversion of this chord presented by the simultaneous sounding of the tonic, fourth (subdominant), sixth, and octave, we find it, as we should expect, slightly less harmonious and pleasing than the former. For while the *fourth* and *sixth* concur in every fourth wave-beat as shown on lines 3, 6, etc., of the tabulation, yet there is no intervening concurrence of the sixth with the tonic, corresponding with that of the dominant in the previous case.

All of this must be accepted as proof that even in the musical scale and common harmony, there is much besides mere chance and that the result is tuneful because it could not logically be anything else.

Note XVII

Accepting now the diatonic scale as something more than accident, let us apply to it one or two of the laws of the geometric measurements, for it must by this time be clearly seen that the laws of sound, like those of all force and motion, are part and parcel of the kingdom of polar force, and we shall find many exact correlations on examining plate 44 which I have prepared for the purpose of illustrating the subject.

With the most accurate mathematical measurement, the relation of the prime circle T^3 to that of the first progression of the equilateral triangle at T^2, by their respective diameters, represents vibratory difference of exactly the octave which we have been studying, while the second progression of the hexagon at D^2 represents the dominant of the same tonic, and this with the utmost nicety and precision, as has been carefully figured by the actual ratios of vibration superimposed upon a trigonometrically calculated diagram of the progressions, thus achieving an accuracy far beyond the limits of the drawing which is nevertheless the only means of illustrating the subject.

Examining the plate we see that the vibratory rate of our supposed tonic is measured by the distance from T^3 on the one side to T^3 at the other end of the diameter of the prime circle, while the vibratory rate of the octave below is measured by the line T^2 to T^2. Inspection shows that this latter is the diameter of the circle of the first progression of the equilateral triangle, and is therefore, as it should be, octant to the T^3 diameter. In order to make the matter clear to the reader without the use of logarithms and all of the paraphernalia of scientific measurements, a scale has been added to the diagram so that it could be put to an illustrative test. Let us substitute the actual note C^3 for our hypothetical tonic. Then by the scale of measurements we shall see that the distance from T^3 to T^3 represents 1056 units of this measure, and this corresponds with the number of vibrations per second necessary to produce the note C^3. Measuring again, we find that from T^2 to T^2 equals 528 of the same units, or just half. This we recognize immediately is the octave below, or C^2. Again measuring we find that from D^2 to D^2 is an almost imperceptible amount less than 800 units, giving us accurately the ocular equivalent of the note G^2 which of course is the dominant of the tonic C^2 and is in fact produced by 793 vibrations per second. We may go further and add between these at M^1 and M^2 the measure of the vibration causing the mediant, by dividing the radius $X-T^1$ into extreme and mean proportion at M^2 or the radius $X-T^2$ into the same ratio at M^1 and so producing the circles representing the mediants E^2 and E^1 for our tonic C. The interesting mathematical accuracy with which these statements are true can only be disclosed by recourse to the dry process of calculation which probably would not interest the reader but which is demonstrable nevertheless. All of the rest of the notes of the present standard diatonic scale might be analyzed with equal interest, but lack of space forbids more than has been shown, and if from this it has been made clear that the laws of pitch are geometric and are persistently similar to those which govern outward form, my object will have been attained.

It should be kept in mind that in studying a musical scale the *vibratory relations* of the various notes are all that are important. The arbitrary standard fixing the number of vibrations which shall be called "A" has no bearing on the subject, since, whatever standard be accepted, the *intervals* would bear the same ratio to each other, each note rising or falling as the standard is higher or lower. Thus the theory governing the vibratory intervals will in all standards be the same. The rapidity of vibration quoted in the statements regarding sound is taken from the English Philharmonic standard, though any other would serve the purpose as well.

Referring again to plate 44, it will be seen that C^3, C^2, and C^1 are correlated by progressions of the equilateral triangle, whereby it is clear that they are precisely octant. Figured mathematically and without regard to music, their vibratory relation to each other would be 1056, 528, and 264, which are their precise musical relations. Examining the relations of the tonic and dominant from a purely mathematical standpoint, and in accordance with the diagram alone, we see that the relation of T^3 and D^2 is established by two progressions of the hexagon. Consulting the table of progressions in Note I, it will be found that the decimal value of two progressions of the hexagon, in terms of the prime radius, is .7500 and applying this mathematically to the Philharmonic standard with which we started we find that the vibratory rapidity of dominant should be, according to the trigonometry of the diagram and regardless of music, 792 vibrations per second, which is exactly the number set by the standard. Again, testing the diagram by the standard, we find that the value of the mediant is set in the plate at the extreme and mean division of the total number of vibrations of the tonic above (T³). This is found to be 653 as against 660 of the standard, a variation of one vibration in every hundred, if measured by the Philharmonic standard. It follows from this that the diagram illustrates all of the notes of the common chord throughout the entire scale with a variation of one vibration per hundred in every third note, the other two notes out of every three being absolutely perfect.

NOTE XVIII

The entire gamut of visible light, and consequently of colour, is contained within an octave of light vibrations. This is clearly shown by the fact that the measurement of the longest visible red ray approximates .00008 cm. while the shortest visible violet averages in the neighbourhood of .00004 cm. both figures being perhaps slightly higher than the ordinary eye will accept. The invisible infra red rays have been measured up to a length four hundred times as great as that stated (.03cm) and the ultra violet have been carried to .00001, being, of course, long vanished from visibility.

Tabulated, the centre of the spectrum bands gives these lengths: Red, .000068cm., yellow, .000058cm, green, .000052cm, blue, .000046cm, and violet, .000042cm.

The use of the term primary colours requires some care. In spectrum analysis, Clerk Maxwell determined that the red, green, and blue were sufficient to produce all the others, including, in toto, white. When used in pigments, however, as in three-colour printing, the primary tones are peacock blue, crimson, and light yellow, and the total product is black.

NOTE XIX

In even so simple a matter as a falling stone, measurements prove many complications which bear upon the final result. Not only has the loss of the eastward motion its influence, but another little thought of factor has its effect as well. Try some day, to drop a stone to the bottom of a deep, unused mine pit. Unless it be very wide and fairly shallow, you will never succeed, without hitting the side first. Barring the slight loss of eastward motion of which I have spoken, your missile will plunge downward on a line straight from its point of release toward the centre of the earth, but during the space of time required for it to reach the bottom, the earth swings along and the pit with it, so that the sides of the pit and the line of descent are no longer parallel, and sooner or later the wall of the excavation will, so to speak, bump sidewise into the dropping stone, which has continued on its original course, all unmindful of the fact that, as Galileo historically and defiantly declared, the earth does move. The movement of the stone has been practically straight down, but, meanwhile, the earth has "side-stepped" and receives the stone from below.

Note XX

I claim no originality for this method of creating a catenary curve, it being shown by a number of engineers and in constant use whenever catenaries are required. It is not a new idea, and we may go back to Dürer and da Vinci and find similar methods in use by them. Compare Dürer's method of drawing an Ionic Volute.

Note XXI

For mere convenience and for the purposes of comparison, I have omitted in the text to refer to the recognized fact that the heavenly bodies are not perfect spheres, so far as known. The form is that of an oblate spheroid, but this oblateness, while a known and ascertained quantity, is nevertheless so slight as to be negligible in such a calculation as any of those in question. In the cases of the Sun, Moon, Mercury, Venus, and the asteroids, it has never even been ascertained. In our earth it is about twenty-six miles in the total diameter, or about one unit in one thousand of circumference, while Mars has slightly larger oblateness, Jupiter, Uranus, and Neptune considerably more. In no case, however, is this sufficient to alter the general statements of the text.

Note XXII

Speaking on the subject of spirals, in his work *Growth and Form*, Dr. d'Arcy Thompson says: "Of several mathematical curves whose form and development may be so conceived (*i. e.*, as spirals) the most important, and the only two with which we shall deal, are those which are known as (1) the equable spiral or spiral of Archimedes, and (2) the logarithmic, or equiangular spiral. The former may be illustrated by the spiral coil in which a sailor coils a rope upon the deck; as the rope is of uniform thickness, so in the whole spiral coil is each whorl of the same breadth as that which precedes it and as that which follows it. Using its ancient definition, we may define it by saying, that "if a straight line revolve uniformly about its extremity, a point which likewise travels uniformly along it will describe the equable spiral."[1] This, it will be noted is the spiral delineated in figure A of plate 62 and, for convenience called the watch spring. Figure B is also the Archimedean spiral from the usual point of illustration. Concerning the golden spiral shown in figure E, something has already been said in Note V, and it may for our purposes be grouped with the logarithmic spirals, as shown in figure F. On the subject of the logarithmic spiral, Dr. Thompson in the work above referred to, has this to say:

"In contrast to this (the Archimedean) is the logarithmic spiral of the Nautilus or the snail-shell, the whorls of which gradually increase in breadth, and do so in a steady and unchanging ratio. Our definition is as follows: 'If, instead of travelling with uniform velocity, our point move along the radius vector with a velocity increasing as the distance from the pole, then the path described is a logarithmic spiral.' Each whorl which the radius vector intersects will be broader than its predecessor in a definite ratio: the radius vector will increase in length in geometrical progression, as it sweeps through successive equal angles; and the equation of the spiral will be $r = a^\theta$. As the spiral of Archimedes, in our example of the coiled rope, might be looked upon as a coiled cylinder, so may a logarithmic spiral, in case of the shell, be pictured as a cone coiled upon itself."

Another spiral of which nothing is said in the text, but which is of interest in any such subject, is what is technically known as the involute of a circle as exemplified in plate 155 below. If we wrap a string around any cylindrical body, near its base, and tie a pencil to the end, the line made by the pencil in unwrapping it from the cylinder will be that shown by the spiral in the diagram, hence its

---

[1] Leslie's *Geometry of Curved Lines*, p. 417. This is practically identical with Archimedes' own definition (ed. Torelli, p. 219).

name, the involute or unwinding of a circle. The process here described is a very useful one and may be put to purpose in mapping any curves, from the cone of a shell to the curves of a piece of ornamental brass, and is in common use in many of the arts and crafts.

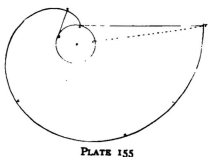

PLATE 155
INVOLUTE OF A CIRCLE

NOTE XXIII

That Dürer was a great student of mathematical forms one need only examine his works to learn. In the fourth book of his Geometrical Institutes, in figures 30, 31, 32, etc., does he not go even into details as to how to construct models of the regular polyhedral angles? I have found space here only for his drawing of the Ionic Volute and his free hand logarithmic spiral, but of almost equal interest are many others of his methods which may be inspected in the pages of his works.

NOTE XXIV

It is no new thing in this world of contraries, that a man should establish a reputation for his work and then go down to posterity under a nickname. In the case of Leonardo of Pisa, fate, with still further irony, decreed that the pseudonym should be derogatory as well. This Fibonacci, son of good, stupid dunce though he was called, rose superior however to this derision and not only collected but originated many useful theorems of science, one of which was the construction of such a succession of numbers as that the sum of any two contiguous ones should equal the next in order. Of such a series, only two exist, the series 0, 1, 1, 2, 3, 5, 8,

13, 21, 34, 55, 89, etc., and the second, 2, 1, 3, 4, 7, 11, 18, 29, 47, 76, etc. The former, however, is the perfectly upward progression and is the one known as the Fibonacci series (also as Lamé's series) and is found constantly exemplified in phyllotaxis. It is to this that reference is here made. Its relation to extreme and mean proportion has been many times referred to in *Nature's Harmonic Unity* and in these pages, where it is seen that, where the mere numbering of parts or wholes is needed, as in counting pips on a pine cone, the Fibonacci series has its myriad uses, but that when exactness and continuous growth are in question, nothing short of the absolutely correct and expansive form of the golden series can be applied.

Note XXV

The works of Lankester, D'Arcy Thompson, *The Challenger Reports*, Cook's *Curves of Life* will serve to fill in where a start is made under Leonardo da Vinci, with writings like Bronn and Simroth and a hundred others en route. The Museum of Natural History in New York and similar institutions in every large city contain collections replete with information. The same is true of other beautiful spiral forms, horns and the like which it would be interesting to go into in more detail, but which the space allotted to this portion of our subject nevertheless forbids.

Note XXVI

The universality of the application of the golden series of extreme and mean proportion in Nature was repeatedly referred to in *Nature's Harmonic Unity* and, in some connections, somewhat exhaustively treated, and need not again be taken up in detail here. The quotations of the text are introduced from the former work and those wishing further to pursue what was there said, are referred to such pages as 63, where we stated that "too much importance can hardly be attributed in a work of this kind to the principle of extreme and mean ratio, for there are few objects in the living forms of Nature which do not reveal its effect, thus declaring the law to be one of the fundamentals of true proportion." The continuous nature of this proportion is explained at pages 285 *et seq.*, *Nature's Harmonic Unity* and the universality is clearly shown on such pages as 181, 182, and many others to which the reader may turn.

Note XXVII

· The continuous relationship between the golden series of extreme and mean
proportion and the human anatomy is so clearly shown in the former work, and,

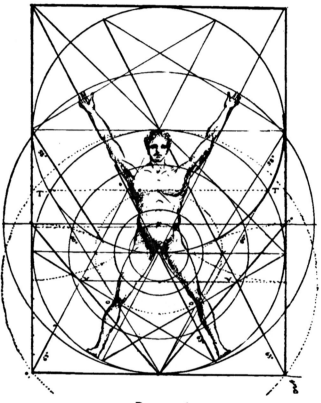

PLATE 156

YOUNG MAN WITH ARMS UPRAISED

I trust, in the illustration presented in Chapter VI, preceding, that little need be
added in the way of reference farther than to reintroduce plate 168 from that work,

which is here shown as plate 156. I will not stop here to go into all of the details shown in this interesting plate, but would lay emphasis on the extremely important fact that the anatomy is shown in its relation to a continuous extreme and mean series of the most pronounced type. The circles are separated from one another by spaces in exact golden proportion and should be compared with plate 117 set in the text of this work. The same facts were further emphasised by plate 169 in the former treatise, in which the divisions of a side figure were explained. Regarding plate 156 (formerly plate 168) a sufficient statement will be that formerly made, as follows: "It will now be found that the upper line of this (extreme and mean) intersects the umbilicus while the lower will mark the extension of the arms at the side. This plate is divided on the lines and arcs necessary for obtaining the mathematically correct extreme and mean ratio as explained in the passage on that subject, and the width of the shoulders, position of the umbilicus, size of the head, and length of the arm will be found to correspond to the rules laid down."

NOTE XXVIII

In summing up the situation, it might briefly be put thus:

(1) Does Nature make free use of such forms as are numbered among the Great Modules?

Answer. The Tetragon Family, with its subdivisions of the equilateral triangle, the square, the hexagon, and octagon, are found in all laws of gravity, light, sound, heat, and other forces, constantly, and also in the formations of crystals, diatoms, and many botanical classes such as the lily. The Family of the Golden Series is found to be represented in every pentagonal flower, of which there are no end; in echinoderms, and, as a measure of proportion and space, is found everywhere, including, as we have seen, nearly every subdivision of the human body. The Spiral group, subdivided into its various classes, has a most important bearing and shows itself not only directly in phyllotaxis, but in every shell, in growth and form of all kinds.

(2) Are these forms geometric?

Answer. They are not merely geometric, but they are the sum of that system set out in the first chapters as the Great Modules.

(3)   Does Nature use them geometrically?

Answer.   Geometry is merely our human means of understanding and classifying certain features of science.   Nature needs none of this written assistance, but, nevertheless, she demonstrates herself along lines which conform to the terms and laws of geometry.

(4)   Has man followed these in creating his best works?

Answer.   When man developed beyond the merest and barest necessities and began to beautify his surroundings, he knew little of mathematics and cared less.   Notwithstanding which, when he drew a charcoal effigy of his fellow man, he attempted to put down what he saw and, since that fellow man was proportioned in geometrical form and the golden series abounded in his structure, the carving or drawing, however rude, was if true, in the same relation.   When he planned a beautiful building, it is evident that he used the structure of flowers and other familiar natural objects in proportioning his spaces, and thus they conformed to the rules as well.   Finally man began to study out the whys and wherefores of all this, and it is this process which we would continue.

Note XXIX

It may safely be said, without fear of contradiction, that of all the Arts, Music is far and away the most mathematically exact, and in this I do not refer to the question of musical "tempo," which is comparatively simple, but to the rules of vibration and tonal production which govern the relationships of the members of the diatonic scale, and the harmony of composition.

Any studious musician will understand that the natural and perfectly constructed scale, true to the ear and to its mathematical proportions of vibration, contains perfect octaves, perfect dominants, mediants, and other intervals, but he will also understand that this natural and perfect scale is *susceptible of no use whatever* in any key except that of the tonic for which it was constructed.   Its tone intervals, as established by the ear and by science, are not all equal, nor are its half tones equal.   For example, the ratio of vibration between the tonic and its second (a whole tone) is not the same as between this second and the mediant (also called a whole tone), for if the perfect scale for a single key be examined, the interval from the tonic to the second will prove to be in proportion to the interval between the second and the dominant in the ratio of 51 : 46 or thereabouts, and *not* according to precise equality. Naturally, then, if the perfect scale based, for example, on "C" as a tonic, be used for the rendition of anything written in the key of "D," it will be found that the interval from this new tonic to its second cannot of course be the perfect first step required, since the interval to be utilised has already been restricted to the vibratory difference indicated for the second step in the "C" scale, to wit, we are obliged to use the smaller of the two so-called whole tones, whereas in this new key of "D" we need the larger whole tone for the first interval. The farther the process is carried, the worse will be found the result, except that every octave is a repetition of every other. The ideal and perfect scale for the tonic "C" thus becomes utterly useless for a modulation into any musically remote key.

To adapt any keyed instrument to general use, therefore, Nature's principle of compromise has been utilised in setting what is technically called an equalised "temperament," the greater intervals representing the greater ratio of difference of vibration, yielding to their lesser neighbours sufficient of their surplus so that all of the so-called whole tones represent equal, or nearly equal ratios of difference, the half tones being treated in the same way, thus leaving no key in its primary perfection at the expense of every other, but permitting all to be alike possible and pleasing. Here, if anywhere, we surely have an example of a universally adopted, measurable variation from mathematical perfection, under a system of compensation which produces a result both artistic and at the same time eminently practical.

From all of these facts it seems clear that, while Beauty is of many kinds and has many exemplars, her form is always controlled by Mother Nature, and if, by studious observation, man can re-learn a few of the principles employed by Nature in the creation of those forms which are universally acknowledged as Beauty, perhaps the determination of what is beautiful in art, music, architecture, and painting may be made simpler, more certain, and less subject to the whim and fancy of temperamental minds and the fluctuating personal equation. (*Music in Nature*, Coan.)

Note XXX

The particulars of the investigations of Viollet-le-Duc, Gwilt, and others on this point have been summarised in *Nature's Harmonic Unity*, and should be consulted at length in the original works of those authors. In this connection it is well to bear in mind the superiority of the golden series over the Fibonacci, when the proportioning of decorations or spaces is in question.

NOTE XXXI

From prehistoric days down to the modern gypsy, national and tribal symbols have abounded, interwoven with those of superstition, mysticism, and religion. Most of these are purely local. A few, however, have attained a wide, even a world wide, significance, among which we may mention the *svastika*, the pentacle, and the cross, the origin and history of all of which are shrouded in mystery. As to the pentacle, some statement has already been made, and regarding the cross, it is well to remember that, like many other emblems adopted by Christianity, it long antedates our religion as a sacred symbol, both the tau-cross and the gammadion or *svastika* being early forms of the same figure. The tau-cross is frequently found in Egypt while the *svastika*, so familiar in India, China, and the Far East is practically never seen in the land of the lotus. Concerning the *svastika*, Thomas M. Fallow, editor of the *Antiquary*, has this to say: "The adoption by early Christians of *svastika* was no doubt influenced by the idea of the occult Christian significance which they thought they recognised and which could be used with special meaning among themselves without at the same time arousing the ill-feeling of those among whom they lived."

This symbol, of which the name is taken from the Sanscrit (Su-well and asti-being) is probably the oldest symbol in continuous use, being found as early as the bronze age. In its general position, with the arms pointing in the direction of the course of the sun, it is universally considered an omen of good fortune, whence, perhaps, its Oriental name. Were we to visit India and study its traditions, a striking example of the use of *svastika* would meet us at Bharahat, a village in the state of Nagod and not far from Allahabad. About three centuries before Christ, there was erected here a Burial Mound or *stupa*, the ground plan and decorated railings of which show the form of a gigantic *svastika*. The archeologist Heinrich Schliemann, discoverer of the sight of Homer's Troy and relentless follower of symbolism from the legendary (or was it real?) Atalantis of the Timæus to the coast of Central America, dug up examples in Asia Minor; coins have been found bearing it; and the collections of Cyprian pottery excavated under the direction of General Louis P. di Cesnola, now resting in the Metropolitan Museum of New York show distinct examples. Central America presents its instances, and the American Indians were not unfamiliar with it and weave it in their Navajo blankets such as many of us use for steamer rugs. I have already referred to Sir Theodore Cook's sketch of this symbol, and W. R. Hall-Caine, W. A. Moore, Heaton Cooper and other authorities on the Isle of Man generally agree in deriving the three-legged symbol of that famous land of Finn MacCoole from this source. In this connection it is interesting to note that the ancient "map of Man, by Cæsar called Mona" and marked as performed by John Speed in 1605 bears the imprint of this symbol in the upper right hand corner, which even then, long anterior to the adoption of the motto *Quocunque jeceris stabit* (which ever way you throw me, I stand) seems to have typified the *Ellan Vannin Veg Veen*.

Note XXXII

In examining the crozier in connection with the fern and volute, it should be noted that the volute is not invariably in the form of a logarithmic spiral, sometimes, as in the case of Dürer's Ionic volute, taking the curves of the Archimedean form instead.

Note XXXIII

It will have been frequently noted that both in *Nature's Harmonic Unity* and in *The Great Modules* a clear distinction was made between those laws of Nature which were found to apply to inorganic forms and to force, on the one hand, and to those which governed growth and vitality on the other,—a distinction which has been emphasised in the present pages. On the same subject, though with entirely different treatment, an interesting work, entitled to consideration, in which these distinctions between fixed forms, the static, and life, the dynamic, has recently been brought out by Jay Hambidge under the title of *Dynamic Symmetry*. Without agreeing to all of the conclusions apparently reached by Mr. Hambidge, a more extended reference to his work would nevertheless have been given herein but for the fact that the present pages were all set up in type, though delayed somewhat by war conditions from publication, before *Dynamic Symmetry* reached the public.

Note XXXIV

No work of the nature of the present one would be complete at this time without a reference to the recent investigations regarding the action of gravity on light lately undertaken under the leadership of Alfred Einstein and received both favourably and unfavourably by the scientific world. But for the fact that the results of these investigations were placed before the public after the present pages were all in type a more analytical reference to them might be made; but, suffice to say, as must be known to almost every reader, that the new stand taken is that the rays of light may be deflected by the influence of gravity, these conclusions being largely based on observations taken during the last vernal solar eclipse. Whether time will prove that the deflection of the star waves observed was caused by heat and other superficial conditions of the solar body itself or by gravity remains to be demonstrated. Meanwhile, the matter remains one of academic interest so far as the conclusions of this book are concerned since such a deflection, whatever its cause or extent, is so minute as to have escaped observation all these centuries and could have no influence on matters of proportion or beauty.

INDEX

CPSIA information can be obtained at www.ICGtesting.com
Printed in the USA
LVOW021206140112

263874LV00007B/19/P